LIFE AND RED FLAGS: A FRAUD EXAMINER'S GUIDE ON NAVIGATING THE LOWS

ANJUL MITTRA

To my parents,Atul & Sheetal and brother,Manul for their unwavering support, love, and belief in me—even when I doubted myself.

To my Dadi, whose love and presence shaped me, and whose loss reminded me of life's deepest lessons.

To my Nani, whose love and presence spoiled me, and whose perseverance reminds me of moving on.

To my colleagues,Chirag & Prem, whose insights, challenges, and camaraderie have shaped my journey, pushing me to grow both personally and professionally.

To my friends[Arjun,Gaurav,Sashi,Bobby,Neel,Nitin & Sharad] and extended family[Mittras,Khannas & Mehras], who have stood by me through every high and low, offering strength, laughter, and perspective.

To my Siblings,[Padmani ,Aakriti,Divyansh,Megha,Mehul,Reshul,Sara] who gave me unconditional love and companionship, proving that the purest bonds leave the greatest impact.

To my pets,[Simba,Fubu,Rambo,Jambo] who gave me unconditional love and companionship, proving that the purest bonds leave the greatest impact.

To my co-founders,[Arijeet & Alok], for their trust & patience in me.

And to everyone who has ever ignored the red flags, justified their struggles, or convinced themselves that they would "fix things later"—this book is for you.

May we all learn to recognize the signs, confront the truth, and reclaim control over our lives.

Contents

Contents

Contents

Foreword

Life is full of red flags—some we see but ignore, some we misinterpret, and some we don't even recognize until they've caused damage. As a fraud examiner, I've spent years uncovering deception in corporate reports, financial statements, and investment deals. But I've come to realize that fraud isn't just something that happens in boardrooms or on balance sheets. It happens in our own lives—in the way we justify bad decisions, avoid uncomfortable truths, and delay taking action.

This book isn't about fraud in the traditional sense. It's about the fraud we commit against ourselves—the lies we believe, the red flags we ignore, and the damage we allow to build up in different areas of our lives. Whether it's our health, relationships, finances, career, or mindset, the principles of fraud examination can help us navigate challenges, uncover blind spots, and regain control.

I know this because I've lived it.

The Red Flags I Ignored

For most of my life, I struggled with obesity. I carried the extra weight not just on my body but in my mind, in the way I saw myself, and in the way I allowed it to shape my experiences. I convinced myself that I was "just built this way," that it wasn't a big deal, that I would lose weight when I was ready. But deep down, I knew I was ignoring the warning signs—the same way someone ignores small financial discrepancies, thinking they won't add up to anything significant.

Then came the moment of truth.

During a trip to South Africa, I tried to get on a ride, excited like everyone else. But when I went to secure the safety harness, it wouldn't fit. The attendant looked at me, shook his head, and told me I couldn't get on.

I felt humiliated, standing there as others moved past me, boarding with ease while I had to step aside. That moment wasn't just about a ride—it was about everything I had been avoiding. It was a reminder that my weight wasn't just a number, it was a limitation. It was keeping me from fully participating in life.

That was the wake-up call I needed.

I lost 30 kgs in 9 months after that experience. Not through crash diets or extreme measures, but through dedication, consistency, and a commitment to change. I approached my health the way I would a fraud investigation—with honesty, discipline, and a plan.

For three years, I kept the weight off. I built habits, stayed active, and felt in control. Until I wasn't.

When Life Throws You Off Course

Losing weight was a challenge, but maintaining it through grief and loss turned out to be an even bigger test.

When my grandmother passed away from dementia, and shortly after, my pet—my constant companion—was gone too, it felt like my world had shifted. The sense of control I had worked so hard to build started slipping away.

At first, it was small things. A missed workout here, a comfort meal there. But small things add up. Grief makes you vulnerable, and in that vulnerability, I ignored the red flags.

I rationalized my choices:

"I've been through so much—I deserve a break."

"One meal won't hurt."

"I'll start again next week."

But that "next week" kept getting pushed further and further away.

In fraud cases, it's rarely one big crime that causes the downfall—it's small manipulations, gradual justifications, tiny compromises that accumulate until the damage is done. That's exactly how I found myself slipping back into old habits.

I saw the weight creeping back, but I told myself I'd fix it later. I believed my own excuses—the same way people believe financial scams because they want them to be true.

What Fraud & Life Have in Common

In fraud detection, we look for patterns. Deception doesn't happen overnight—it's built over time through small choices, intentional or not. The same applies to life.

When we ignore warning signs in our health, relationships, finances, or careers, we are allowing small issues to snowball into bigger problems. We see the signs, but we rationalize them:

A toxic relationship where the red flags were always there.

A career that feels stagnant, but we convince ourselves it's "fine for now."

A financial decision we know is risky, but we take the gamble anyway.

By the time the damage is evident, it's much harder to fix.

But here's the good news: the moment you recognize the red flags, you have the power to change the outcome.

Life Auditing – A Fraud Examiner's Approach to Living Smarter

What if we audited our own lives the way we audit financial statements?

What if we regularly checked:

Our habits – Are we making choices that support our well-being?

Our relationships – Are the people in our lives lifting us up or holding us back?

Our finances – Are we being mindful of where our money is going?

Our mindset – Are we stuck in negative patterns without realizing it?

Fraud prevention isn't about fixing a problem after it happens—it's about recognizing risks early and putting safeguards in place to prevent bigger damage. Life should be approached the same way.

That's what this book is about.

Why I Wrote This Book

I wrote this book because:

I know what it's like to ignore red flags. I've been there, believing I had control, only to realize I had let things spiral.

I believe in practical, structured solutions. Many self-help books give vague advice. But fraud examination has a system—one that can be applied to real life.

We can't afford to wait for a crisis. Small problems, if unchecked, turn into big problems. The sooner we recognize them, the sooner we can change course.

Each chapter will focus on a different area of life—health, relationships, finances, career, decision-making, and more—and provide practical tools for spotting red flags, correcting course, and building a system that prevents self-sabotage.

You'll see real-life examples, my own experiences, and actionable strategies that you can apply immediately.

Your First Audit Starts Now

The greatest fraud we fall for is the lie we tell ourselves—that we have more time, that we'll fix things later, that the warning signs aren't that serious.

But if you've ever ignored a red flag, made an excuse, or found yourself stuck in patterns that hold you back—then you already know that's not true.

You wouldn't ignore financial fraud if it was draining your bank account—so why ignore the red flags that are draining your health, happiness, and future?

This book is about taking a fraud examiner's mindset and applying it to life—so you can identify risks before they turn into crises, make informed decisions, and take back control.

It's time to audit your life and navigate the lows with clarity, strength, and resilience.

Now, let's begin.

Preface

When I first set out to write this book, I wasn't thinking about fraud. I wasn't thinking about corporate scams, Ponzi schemes, or the deceptive financial practices I've spent years analyzing. I was thinking about life—the ups and downs, the decisions we make, the setbacks we endure, and the lessons we often learn too late.

It wasn't until I looked back at my own journey—through struggles with weight, grief, career choices, and personal growth—that I realized something: life has red flags, just like fraud does. The same way financial fraud sneaks up on companies through unchecked risks, personal setbacks often come from ignored warning signs, misplaced trust, and self-deception.

The more I reflected, the more I saw the parallels. In my work as a fraud examiner, I've seen how people fall for scams—not because they're naive, but because they want to believe in the illusion. They overlook inconsistencies, trust the wrong people, and convince themselves that things will work out. I realized that I had done the same thing in different areas of my life.

I ignored red flags in my health until I was denied entry on a ride in South Africa.

I ignored red flags in my emotions until grief sent me back into old, unhealthy habits.

I ignored red flags in my decisions until small missteps turned into bigger setbacks.

We all do this at some point—whether it's in relationships, careers, money, or mental health. And just like fraud, these issues don't happen overnight. They build up slowly, in the background, until they can no longer be ignored.

That's why I wrote this book.

What This Book is About

Life & Red Flags: A Fraud Examiner's Guide on Navigating the Lows is not a self-help book filled with vague inspiration. It's a practical guide that takes lessons from fraud investigation and applies them to real-life challenges.

Each chapter focuses on a different aspect of life—health, finances, relationships, decision-making, career, and more—and explores:

✓? The warning signs we often ignore

✓? Why we deceive ourselves into making bad choices

✓? How to audit our lives and recognize the truth

✓? Strategies to prevent setbacks before they happen

Think of this book as a life audit manual—a structured way to analyze your habits, recognize risks, and put safeguards in place to avoid repeated mistakes.

Who This Book is For

This book is for anyone who has ever ignored a red flag—whether it was about your health, a relationship, a financial decision, or something else entirely.

If you've ever made excuses instead of taking action, this book is for you.

If you've ever trusted the wrong person or situation, this book is for you.

If you've ever found yourself in the same bad cycle, wondering how you got there again, this book is for you.

No matter where you are in life, understanding how to recognize and respond to red flags will help you make better decisions, avoid unnecessary setbacks, and take control of your future.

How to Read This Book

You don't have to read this book in order. Each chapter is designed to stand alone as a guide for different aspects of life.

However, if you want to fully audit your life, I recommend starting with the first few chapters, which set the foundation for understanding self-deception, decision-making, and risk assessment. From there, you can dive into the chapters that resonate with you the most.

At the end of each chapter, you'll find:

? Reflection questions to help you assess your own experiences

? Action steps to start making changes immediately

? Case studies—both personal and professional—illustrating how red flags manifest in different situations

My Personal Journey & Why This Book Matters

I have always been a logical person. In my work, I analyze fraud based on evidence, patterns, and facts. But when it came to my own life, I wasn't always that objective.

For most of my life, I struggled with weight issues, but I didn't take real action . That was my audit failure—the moment the truth became undeniable.

I lost 30 kgs in 9 months, determined to change. And for three years, I stayed disciplined. I had mastered control—or so I thought.

Then, life happened.

When I lost my grandmother to dementia, and shortly after, my pet passed away, my emotional stability crumbled. I started making small excuses—comfort eating, skipping workouts, pushing "health" to the back of my mind. And just like that, the weight started coming back.

At first, I told myself it wasn't a big deal. That I'd fix it later. But that's exactly how financial fraud works—it starts small, and before you know it, the damage is done.

I knew I had two choices:

Keep ignoring the warning signs and let things spiral.

Conduct a life audit, acknowledge where I went wrong, and take back control.

I chose the second option. And through that process, I realized that this mindset—this structured, fraud-examiner approach—could apply to all areas of life.

Final Thoughts: Red Flags Are Warnings, Not Endings

Here's the truth: Red flags don't mean failure. They mean there's still time to change course.

A company that catches fraud early can recover.
A person who recognizes their bad habits can make a shift.
A relationship that spots toxic patterns can be saved—or ended for the right reasons.

The key is awareness and action.

So as you read this book, don't just look for red flags in the examples and case studies—look for them in your own life.

Because the sooner you recognize the warning signs, the sooner you can take control.

Physical Health & Well-being: The Silent Fraud We Commit Against Ourselves

CHAPTER ONE

THE CONCEPT OF SELF-FRAUD IN HEALTH

1.1 The Nature of Fraud and How It Relates to Health

Fraud is a word that carries weight. When we think of fraud, we often picture financial scams, corporate embezzlement, or identity theft—situations where someone deceives others for personal gain. Society condemns fraudsters because their actions cause harm, sometimes irreparable, to unsuspecting victims.

But what if I told you that one of the most damaging frauds of all is one we commit against ourselves?

Unlike financial fraud, where someone else benefits from deception, self-fraud in health has no winners. We deceive ourselves into believing that we're doing fine, that our habits aren't that bad, and that we can always fix things later. We rationalize, justify, and procrastinate until the consequences finally catch up with us—and by then, the damage is often severe.

What is Self-Fraud in Health?

Self-fraud in health is the deliberate self-deception we engage in to avoid taking responsibility for our well-being. It manifests in many ways:

Procrastinating on fitness goals, always saying, "I'll start on Monday."

Believing that occasional healthy meals cancel out weeks of bad eating.

Justifying chronic stress and lack of sleep as a necessity for success.

Ignoring warning signs from our body, thinking they'll go away on their own.

Unlike financial fraud, where the victim might be reimbursed, self-fraud carries no refunds. The price we pay comes in the form of poor health, chronic diseases, lost opportunities, and a diminished quality of life.

1.2 Why We Are Both the Scammers and the Victims

One of the most dangerous aspects of self-fraud is that we don't even realize we're doing it. Unlike an external scam, where someone else deceives us, in health, we play both roles—the scammer and the victim.

The Psychology Behind Self-Deception

Why do we lie to ourselves about our health? The answer lies in several psychological principles:

1. Cognitive Dissonance

Cognitive dissonance is the discomfort we feel when our actions don't align with our beliefs. For example, if we believe we value health but continue eating junk food and avoiding exercise, we experience mental tension. Instead of changing our habits, we often change our perception to reduce this discomfort. This leads to statements like:

"One cheat meal won't hurt."

"I walk a lot at work, so that counts as exercise."

"I don't have time for self-care right now."

Rather than facing the truth—that we're harming our health—we create justifications to maintain our comfort.

2. Future Discounting (The "Later" Mentality)

People tend to discount the value of future rewards in favor of immediate gratification. We know that eating healthy and exercising will benefit us in the long run, but since the negative consequences of poor health don't show up immediately, we prioritize comfort over discipline.

This is why many people only take action after a wake-up call—such as a heart attack, a diabetes diagnosis, or a loved one's health scare.

3. Confirmation Bias

We naturally seek out information that supports our existing beliefs. If we don't want to believe that our habits are harmful, we look for studies, articles, or anecdotes that reinforce our denial. For example:

People who don't exercise might highlight a story about someone who lived to 100 without working out.

People who eat poorly might find an article questioning the science of nutrition.

This selective exposure to information allows us to continue self-deception without guilt.

1.3 Personal Reflection: Have You Been Defrauding Yourself?

Now that we understand the concept of self-fraud in health, it's time to reflect. Take a moment to answer these questions honestly:

Your Relationship with Health

Do you frequently tell yourself you'll start a healthy habit "next week" or "next month"?

When you indulge in unhealthy foods, do you tell yourself, "I deserve this" to justify it?

Do you believe you function well on less sleep, despite feeling tired often?

Have you ignored minor health symptoms, hoping they'll go away?

Do you feel uncomfortable when people talk about fitness or nutrition because it reminds you of what you're neglecting?

Your Daily Health Choices

How many days a week do you engage in intentional physical activity?

When was the last time you had a full night of high-quality sleep?

Do you eat mindfully, or do you tend to snack while distracted?

How often do you feel stressed or overwhelmed without taking steps to manage it?

Have you ever said, "I don't have time for self-care," while spending hours on social media or watching TV?

Facing the Truth

If you answered yes to several of these questions, it's a sign that you may be engaging in self-fraud when it comes to your health. The good news? Now that you recognize the deception, you can start to break free from it.

One of the hardest but most liberating realizations is that no one is coming to save us—our health is entirely our responsibility. We don't need permission to change, and we don't need to wait for a crisis to start taking care of ourselves.

How Self-Fraud Affects Different Aspects of Health

<u>1. Physical Health</u>

Self-fraud in physical health leads to a gradual decline in energy, mobility, and overall vitality. When we neglect our bodies, we experience:

Weight gain and muscle loss.

Increased risk of chronic diseases (diabetes, heart disease, hypertension).

Loss of stamina and endurance.

Higher susceptibility to injuries.

<u>2. Mental Health</u>

Many people don't realize that neglecting physical health has direct consequences on mental well-being:

Poor nutrition and lack of exercise contribute to anxiety and depression.

Chronic stress increases cortisol levels, leading to emotional instability.

Sleep deprivation affects cognitive function, focus, and mood.

<u>3. Financial Health</u>

Ignoring health becomes expensive in the long run. Medical bills, prescription medications, and treatment costs add up. Many people end up spending thousands of dollars treating preventable diseases.

Would you rather invest in a gym membership, healthy food, and preventive care now, or pay for hospital stays, surgeries, and medications later?

The First Step to Ending the Fraud: Acknowledgment

Most people live in denial about their health until a wake-up call forces them to take action. But what if you could make the change before hitting rock bottom?

The Power of Honesty

To truly improve our health, we must stop sugarcoating our habits.

Instead of saying:

? "I don't have time to work out,"

? Say: "I'm not making exercise a priority right now."

? "I can't afford to eat healthy,"

? Say: "I'm choosing to spend my money elsewhere."

These shifts in language force us to take responsibility. When we stop lying to ourselves, we gain the power to change.

The Next Step: Awareness and Action

Keep a health journal for one week—track your food, movement, sleep, and stress levels.

Identify patterns of self-fraud—what excuses come up repeatedly?

Make one small change today, whether it's drinking more water, walking for 15 minutes, or getting an extra hour of sleep.

Final Thoughts: Breaking the Cycle

Self-fraud in health is an epidemic. But unlike financial fraud, which often leaves victims powerless, you have the ability to stop this deception at any moment. The first step is recognizing the problem; the next step is taking action.

In the following sections, we'll explore the specific health lies we tell ourselves and provide actionable strategies to break free. Because the truth is:

Your health is the one investment that never loses value—but only if you stop deceiving yourself and start prioritizing it.

The fraud ends today. Let's move forward together.

CHAPTER TWO

THE MOST COMMON HEALTH LIES WE BELIEVE

We all want to believe we are doing our best when it comes to our health. But deep down, we also know there are things we avoid addressing—excuses we tell ourselves to justify bad habits. These justifications become a web of self-deception that keeps us stuck in unhealthy cycles.In this section, we will uncover the most common health lies people believe and how they prevent us from living optimally. More importantly, we will expose the truth behind these lies and provide practical solutions to break free from them.

2.1 Lie #1: "I Don't Have Time for Exercise"

This is one of the most common health lies people tell themselves. In a world where work hours are long, schedules are packed, and digital distractions consume our free time, exercise is often pushed to the bottom of the priority list.

Why This Lie is Dangerous

By saying we don't have time for exercise, we are essentially saying:

"My health is not important enough to prioritize."

"I will deal with the consequences later."

The truth?

We do have time—it's just not a priority.

You Don't Need Hours in the Gym

Many people assume that getting fit requires a gym membership and hours of workouts. This is a myth. In reality, small bursts of movement throughout the day can be just as effective.

Real-life Examples

Barack Obama made time for a 45-minute workout daily despite running an entire country.

Richard Branson credits morning exercise for increasing his productivity.

Busy parents who integrate play-based workouts (playing tag with their kids, quick home workouts) see tremendous benefits.

Actionable Steps to Break Free from This Lie

? Start with 10-minute workouts—science shows that short bursts of exercise (HIIT, bodyweight circuits) are highly effective.

? Incorporate movement into daily life—take the stairs, park farther away, do squats while brushing your teeth.

? Set a non-negotiable time—just like meetings, schedule workouts and commit.

2.2 Lie #2: "I Eat Healthy... Most of the Time"

Many people convince themselves they have a "mostly" healthy diet, yet their habits tell a different story. The reality is that the modern food industry has made it easy to believe we are eating well when we are not.

Why This Lie is Dangerous

It gives a false sense of security while unhealthy eating patterns persist.

It prevents people from making real changes because they believe they are already doing enough.

The Truth

Hidden Unhealthy Habits

Even those who think they eat healthily often fall into traps:

Relying on "healthy" processed foods (protein bars, fruit juices, flavored yogurts—many packed with hidden sugars).

Underestimating portion sizes—overeating "healthy" food still leads to weight gain.

Mindless snacking—eating while watching TV, scrolling on the phone, or out of boredom.

Actionable Steps to Break Free from This Lie

? Track your food intake for one week—you'll be surprised by the hidden calories and unhealthy patterns.

? Read labels carefully—sugar, trans fats, and artificial ingredients lurk in many so-called "healthy" foods.

? Follow the 80/20 rule—80% whole, unprocessed foods, 20% indulgence in moderation.

2.3 Lie #3: "I Function Well on Little Sleep"

How many times have you heard someone proudly say, "I only need five hours of sleep!"? In our fast-paced world, sleep deprivation is worn like a badge of honor—a symbol of productivity. But the science tells a different story.

Why This Lie is Dangerous

Chronic sleep deprivation affects hormones, metabolism, and mental health.

It lowers cognitive function, making you less productive despite working longer hours.

It increases the risk of obesity, heart disease, and early death.

The Truth

You're Functioning at Half Capacity

Studies show that sleep-deprived individuals perform tasks as poorly as drunk individuals.

A 2017 study linked poor sleep to weight gain due to hormone imbalances.

Lack of sleep causes cravings for junk food, making healthy eating harder.

Actionable Steps to Break Free from This Lie

? Create a nighttime routine—dim lights, limit screen time, and wind down with relaxing activities.

? Track your sleep using wearable devices (smartwatches, apps).

? Prioritize sleep just as you would your work meetings or workouts.

2.4 Lie #4: "Stress is Just a Part of Life"

Modern culture normalizes stress. We tell ourselves that stress is unavoidable and that high levels of anxiety, overworking, and exhaustion are just a part of life.

Why This Lie is Dangerous

Chronic stress is linked to inflammation, heart disease, diabetes, and immune system suppression.

It ages the body faster and contributes to long-term mental health disorders.

Many people don't even realize they are constantly in a stress state.

The Truth

Stress Can Be Managed

Some stress is normal, but chronic stress should not be ignored.

The body can be trained to handle stress more effectively through proper habits.

Small daily stress-reduction techniques can make a huge difference.

Actionable Steps to Break Free from This Lie

? Adopt stress-reducing activities—meditation, breathing exercises, walks in nature.

? Identify and eliminate unnecessary stressors—toxic people, unrealistic workloads.

? Get professional help if needed—therapy and coaching can provide coping strategies.

2.5 Lie #5: "I'll Start When I Feel Motivated"

Many people delay improving their health because they wait for motivation. But motivation is fleeting—discipline and consistency create real change.

Why This Lie is Dangerous

If you wait for motivation, you will never start.

People who rely on motivation tend to quit when it fades.

The Truth

Action Creates Motivation, Not the Other Way Around

Momentum builds motivation. Small wins lead to bigger successes.

Starting with action (even when unmotivated) creates a habit.

Discipline beats motivation every time.

Actionable Steps to Break Free from This Lie

? Start small—just do something. Even a five-minute workout counts.

? Create habits, not goals. Instead of aiming for weight loss, commit to a daily 30-minute walk.

? Use external accountability. Join a class, get a coach, or have a workout partner.

Conclusion: Exposing the Lies and Taking Control

We all tell ourselves health lies at some point. The key is to recognize them, challenge them, and replace them with truth.

? Lie #1: "I don't have time for exercise." → Truth: "I can prioritize movement in my daily life."

? Lie #2: "I eat healthy most of the time." → Truth: "I need to track my diet and make conscious food choices."

? Lie #3: "I function well on little sleep." → Truth: "Quality sleep is non-negotiable for peak performance."

? Lie #4: "Stress is just a part of life." → Truth: "I can control and reduce my stress through intentional habits."
? Lie #5: "I'll start when I feel motivated." → Truth: "Discipline and action create motivation, not the other way around."

Your health is the foundation of everything else in your life. Stop deceiving yourself. Take action today.

CHAPTER THREE

THE REAL COST OF SELF-DECEPTION

Most of us deceive ourselves about our health because the consequences are not immediate. If eating one unhealthy meal instantly led to a heart attack or skipping a single workout made us gain 10 pounds overnight, we would be far more cautious.

But this is not how health works. The damage accumulates slowly—over months, years, and decades—until suddenly, the cost is undeniable.

Self-deception in health has three primary costs:

Financial costs – Rising medical expenses, insurance costs, and lost earnings.

Emotional & mental health costs – Declining self-confidence, stress, and anxiety.

Quality of life costs – A body that limits your experiences, relationships, and freedom.

In this section, we will break down each of these hidden costs and how they manifest in ways most people fail to recognize—until it's too late.

3.1 Financial Costs of Neglecting Health

The Silent Economic Drain of Poor Health

Many people think investing in health is expensive—but they fail to realize that neglecting health is even more costly.

<u>Here's how poor health drains your finances:</u>

Medical Bills – Hospital visits, medications, surgeries, and specialist appointments add up over time.

Lost Productivity – Frequent sick days, decreased work performance, and burnout impact earnings.

Higher Insurance Costs – Health conditions lead to increased premiums and long-term medical expenses.

Long-Term Disability Costs – Chronic diseases often result in loss of income, forcing early retirement or limiting career opportunities.

<u>Case Study: The Lifetime Cost of Diabetes</u>

Consider the case of someone who develops Type 2 diabetes due to poor lifestyle choices. The estimated lifetime cost of managing diabetes includes:

$16,000–$25,000 per year in medication, insulin, doctor visits, and complications.

Indirect costs such as lost wages due to illness, lower work productivity, and increased insurance costs.

Total lifetime cost: Over $500,000+ in preventable expenses.

Compare this to the cost of preventive health habits:

Gym membership: $30–$100 per month

Nutritious meal prep: $50–$100 per week

Preventive check-ups: A few hundred dollars per year

The ROI on health investment is staggering, yet many people refuse to see the long-term financial benefits of prioritizing well-being.

<u>Actionable Steps to Avoid These Costs</u>

? Budget for health the way you budget for necessities. Treat gym memberships, meal prep, and regular check-ups as essential expenses.

? Invest in prevention, not treatment. Spend on fitness, nutrition, and stress management before chronic conditions develop.

? Get health insurance early. The younger and healthier you are, the lower your premiums.

3.2 Emotional & Mental Health Costs

<u>The Hidden Mental Toll of Poor Physical Health</u>

Many people assume physical health is separate from mental well-being. In reality, they are deeply interconnected.

How Poor Physical Health Affects Mental Health

Chronic fatigue reduces motivation and makes daily tasks feel overwhelming.

Poor nutrition contributes to anxiety and depression by affecting neurotransmitters like serotonin and dopamine.

Lack of exercise increases stress and worsens mood disorders.

Body image issues can lead to low self-esteem, social withdrawal, and reduced confidence.

<u>Case Study: The Link Between Obesity & Depression</u>

Research shows that obesity increases the risk of depression by 55%. The cycle looks like this:

Unhealthy eating and lack of exercise → Weight gain.

Weight gain → Negative self-image & decreased confidence.

Low self-esteem → Isolation & avoidance of social interactions.

Isolation → Increased stress, leading to emotional eating & further weight gain.

Why Self-Deception Worsens Mental Health

Many people tell themselves:

"I'm fine, I'll deal with my health later."

"I don't have time for self-care."

"I'll be happier once I lose weight, so I'll wait until then."

The problem? Neglecting health doesn't just affect your body—it also steals your joy, confidence, and ability to fully engage in life.

Actionable Steps to Protect Mental Health

? Make physical activity a daily habit. Exercise releases endorphins, improving mood and reducing stress.

? Prioritize high-quality nutrition. Omega-3s, leafy greens, and whole foods support brain function.

?Seek support. Therapy, fitness communities, or even an accountability partner can make a huge difference.

3.3 Quality of Life Costs

The Gradual Decline That Limits Your Life

The most devastating cost of self-deception is the slow but inevitable decline in life experiences.When you are young, you may not feel the consequences of poor health choices, but over time, your body begins to betray you:

You wake up tired every morning, even after a full night's sleep.

You avoid active vacations because you don't have the stamina to enjoy them.

You struggle with chronic aches and pains that once seemed temporary.

You miss out on playing with your children or grandchildren because movement is difficult.

Case Study: The Cost of Inaction

A 35-year-old man neglects exercise and healthy eating.

By 45, he has gained weight, lost mobility, and developed chronic back pain.

By 55, he is on multiple medications for high blood pressure, diabetes, and cholesterol.

By 65, he struggles with basic activities like climbing stairs or walking long distances.

Compare this to someone who prioritized their health at 35:

Maintains a strong, mobile body well into their 60s, 70s, and beyond.

Can travel, explore, and stay independent without relying on medication or mobility aids.

<u>Actionable Steps to Protect Your Future</u>

? Think about your future self. The habits you build today determine the quality of life you'll have in 10, 20, or 30 years.

? Move every day. Your muscles, joints, and bones depend on regular movement to stay strong.

? Adopt a longevity mindset. Health is not about how you look—it's about how long and how well you can live.

<u>Final Thoughts: The Ultimate Price of Self-Deception</u>

Self-deception about health comes with three undeniable costs:

Financial loss – Medical bills, lost wages, and rising insurance costs.

Emotional suffering – Anxiety, depression, and declining self-confidence.

Diminished quality of life – Missed experiences, reduced independence, and physical limitations.

The Turning Point: Awareness + Action = Transformation

Now that you're aware of the real costs of ignoring your health, the next step is to take action.

? Don't wait until a health crisis forces you to change.

? Start now—small steps, daily choices, and long-term commitment make all the difference.

<u>Key Takeaways from Section 3</u>

✓? The cost of ignoring health is far greater than the cost of maintaining it.

✓? Your mental health is directly linked to your physical well-being.

✓? The choices you make today determine the quality of life you'll have in the future.

✓? It's never too late to make a change—but the earlier you start, the better your outcome.

The silent fraud must end. The best time to take control of your health was years ago. The second-best time is today.

CHAPTER FOUR

How to Stop Defrauding Yourself

At this point, you understand how self-deception sabotages your health and the real costs of inaction. Now comes the most critical question:

? What are you going to do about it?

It's easy to read this and feel momentary motivation, but real change requires more than just awareness—it requires deliberate action. This section will guide you through the process of:

Recognizing the patterns of self-deception.

Creating a system for accountability and progress.

Building sustainable habits for lifelong health.

This isn't about extreme diets or unrealistic fitness goals. It's about making real, lasting changes that will transform your physical and mental well-being.

4.1 Radical Ownership: Taking Responsibility for Your Health

<u>The Hard Truth: No One is Coming to Save You</u>

Too many people wait for external motivation, a perfect time, or a health scare before they take action. The problem? There will never be a perfect time.

? You must take full ownership of your health. No one else can do it for you.

Instead of saying:

"I don't have time to exercise." → Say: "I haven't made exercise a priority yet."

"Healthy eating is too expensive." → Say: "I choose to spend my money elsewhere."

"I just don't have the motivation." → Say: "I need to build habits that don't rely on motivation."

<u>Case Study: The Power of Ownership</u>

James, a 42-year-old businessman, struggled with weight gain and chronic fatigue. He blamed his stressful job and lack of time. After a minor heart attack, he realized that his excuses were costing him his life. By shifting his mindset to radical ownership, he:

? Stopped waiting for time and created time for workouts.

? Took control of his diet instead of blaming his busy schedule.

? Started seeing his health as an investment, not an inconvenience.

<u>Actionable Steps to Take Ownership Today</u>

? Write down your biggest health excuses. Challenge them with honest alternatives.

? Identify your "why." Why do you want better health? Long life? More energy? Confidence?

? Make a commitment—stop waiting for external motivation and take action now.

4.2 The 1% Rule: Small Daily Improvements for Massive Results

Why Small Changes Matter More Than Big Goals

Most people fail at improving their health because they aim too big, too fast. They:

Try to work out for an hour daily after years of inactivity.

Attempt extreme diets that they can't sustain.

Expect immediate results and quit when progress is slow.

Instead, the 1% Rule suggests that tiny, consistent improvements are far more effective than radical overhauls.

? 1% improvement every day compounds into massive transformation over time.

Example: The Power of 1% Daily Change

Walking 5 minutes per day adds up to over 30 hours of movement per year.

Cutting one sugary drink per day results in 15–20 lbs of weight loss per year.

Sleeping 30 minutes earlier each night significantly improves brain function and energy.

<u>Actionable Steps to Implement the 1% Rule</u>

? Pick one small, realistic habit to change today.

? Make it so easy you can't fail. (E.g., do one push-up, walk for two minutes.)

? Increase slowly. After a week, add 1–2% more effort.

4.3 Building an Accountability System

<u>Why Willpower Alone is Not Enough</u>

Willpower is a limited resource—if you rely solely on self-control, you will eventually fail. Instead, external accountability and systems ensure long-term success.

Types of Accountability That Work

? Public Commitment: Announce your goal to friends, family, or social media.

? Accountability Partners: Find someone with similar health goals and check in regularly.

? Professional Help: Hire a coach, trainer, or nutritionist.

? Tracking Systems: Use apps or journals to monitor progress.

<u>Case Study: How External Accountability Changed Mark's Life</u>

Mark, a 35-year-old corporate employee, struggled with consistency. He started using:

A fitness tracking app to log workouts.

A weekly check-in system with a friend.

A rewards system—after completing 30 workouts, he treated himself to a weekend getaway.

Within six months, he lost 20 lbs and built sustainable habits without relying on willpower alone.

<u>Actionable Steps to Build Accountability</u>

? Find an accountability partner or group.

? Start tracking progress—weight, meals, workouts, or habits.

? Use a reward system to stay motivated.

4.4 Overcoming Obstacles & Setbacks

What Happens When You Fail? (Because You Will)

Every health journey comes with setbacks—missed workouts, bad eating days, or motivation dips. The key is not avoiding failure but learning to recover quickly.

The All-or-Nothing Trap

One of the biggest reasons people quit is perfectionism. They think:

"I missed one workout, so I might as well skip the week."

"I ate badly today, so my diet is ruined."

This all-or-nothing mindset is destructive. Instead, adopt the 80/20 approach—consistency over perfection.

How to Bounce Back Quickly

? Expect failure. No one is perfect, and mistakes are part of progress.

? Use the "Never Miss Twice" Rule. If you miss one day, get back on track immediately.

? Keep a "Reset Plan" ready. Have a go-to strategy for getting back on track (e.g., drink water, do a quick workout, or prepare a healthy meal).

Case Study: How Sarah Stopped Quitting After Setbacks

Sarah, a 29-year-old professional, constantly fell off her diet whenever she had one bad eating day. She learned to:

? Forgive herself for slip-ups.

? Return to good habits immediately instead of waiting for Monday.

? Focus on long-term progress, not short-term perfection.

Final Thoughts: The Fraud Ends Today

Your Future Self is Watching

Every decision you make today—whether to work out or skip it, to eat whole foods or processed junk—creates your future self.

? You can continue deceiving yourself, delaying action, and paying the price later.

? Or you can take control now and experience more energy, confidence, and a longer life.

Your Next Step

Instead of reading this and moving on, commit to one action right now:

Write down ONE small habit you will start today.

Find an accountability partner.

Set a simple goal for the next seven days.

? Remember: Success in health isn't about perfection—it's about consistent progress.

The fraud ends now. The real transformation begins today.

Key Takeaways from Section 4

✓? Health ownership is a choice—you have the power to change.

✓? Small, daily improvements create massive long-term success.

✓? Accountability and tracking prevent failure.

✓? Perfection isn't necessary—consistency is what matters.

The only question left: Are you ready to take action?

CHAPTER FIVE

FINAL THOUGHTS: THE FRAUD ENDS TODAY

If you've read this far, you already know the truth:

? You've been deceiving yourself about your health.

? You've justified bad habits with clever excuses.

? You've delayed action because the consequences weren't immediate.

But now, you can't unsee the truth. The fraud has been exposed, and *you have a decision to make:*

Ignore everything you've learned and continue down the path of self-neglect, hoping you'll "get lucky" with your health.

Or

Acknowledge the deception, take responsibility, and start making real changes today.

The choice is yours. But remember this: Every day you delay, the cost of inaction increases.

The Moment of Decision: Are You Ready to Stop Lying to Yourself?

Most people will never take action on their health until something forces them to:

A doctor tells them they have high blood pressure or diabetes.

They experience a health scare, like a stroke or heart attack.

They wake up one day and realize they can't physically do the things they used to enjoy.

But why wait for a crisis to take control of your life?

The truth is, you don't need a wake-up call—you already have one right now.

<u>The Harsh Truth No One Wants to Admit</u>

If you continue your current habits, where will you be in 5 years?

If you ignore your health, will you have the energy and mobility to enjoy life in 10 years?

If you don't change, will you regret the opportunities and experiences you missed because you felt sluggish, tired, or sick?

The answer is clear: The cost of inaction is far greater than the discomfort of change.

<u>What Will Your Future Self Say About the Choices You Make Today?</u>

Imagine yourself 10, 20, or 30 years from now.

One version of you:

? Overweight, constantly tired, relying on medication.

? Limited mobility, unable to enjoy simple activities.

? Regretful, wishing you had made different choices when you had the chance.

Another version of you:

? Healthy, energetic, and able to travel, play with grandkids, and enjoy life.

? Independent, free from preventable diseases and medication.

? Confident, happy, and living at your full potential.

The only difference? The decisions you make today.

<u>The "All-or-Nothing" Trap: Why Perfection is Not Required</u>

Many people fail at improving their health because they fall into the perfection trap. They believe:

"If I can't work out every day, I might as well not start."

"If I mess up my diet once, the whole week is ruined."

"If I don't see immediate results, it's not worth it."

But real health transformation is not about being perfect—it's about being consistent.

? Progress, not perfection, is the key to lifelong health.

How to Avoid the Perfection Trap

? Stop waiting for the "perfect time"—start today, even if it's just one small change.

? Accept that setbacks will happen—focus on getting back on track, not being perfect.

? Remember that consistency beats intensity—small daily actions matter more than extreme efforts.

<u>Your Action Plan: How to End the Fraud Today</u>

The key to breaking free from self-deception is taking immediate action. Here's a simple plan to start:

Step 1: Identify Your Biggest Self-Deception

Write down the top excuse or lie you've been telling yourself about your health.

Examples:

"I don't have time to exercise."

"I eat healthy most of the time."

"I'll start next week."

Now, rewrite that excuse with honesty:

? "I don't have time to exercise."

? "I haven't made exercise a priority, but I can start small today."

Step 2: Pick One Small Habit to Change Today

Instead of trying to change everything at once, start with one simple habit that is so easy you can't fail.

Examples:

Drink one extra glass of water.

Take a 5-minute walk.

Replace one unhealthy meal with a whole-food option.

Sleep 30 minutes earlier.

Step 3: Set a 7-Day Challenge for Yourself

Challenge yourself to stick to your small habit for just one week.

No long-term commitment.

No drastic changes.

Just 7 days of consistency.

At the end of the week, reflect:

Did you feel better?

Was the change easier than expected?

What's the next small habit you can add?

This gradual approach prevents burnout and builds long-term success.

<u>Why This Time Will Be Different</u>

You've probably tried to improve your health before. Maybe you've started diets, workout routines, or lifestyle changes—but eventually, you fell back into old habits.

So why will this time be different?

Because this time, you're not following a program—you're changing the way you think about health.

? This time, you're taking full responsibility.

? This time, you're not looking for quick fixes—you're building lifelong habits.

? This time, you're making a decision that your future self will thank you for.

<u>Final Thoughts: The Power of Choosing Yourself</u>

At the end of the day, health is about choice.

You can:

? Continue deceiving yourself and paying the price later.

? Choose to take control, no matter where you are right now.

You don't need permission. You don't need motivation. You just need to decide.

? The fraud ends today. ?

? The transformation begins now. ?

Are you ready?

Take the first step—right now. ?

<u>Key Takeaways from This Chapter</u>

✓? Stop waiting for a perfect time—there isn't one.

✓? Perfection isn't required—consistency is.

✓? One small habit change today will create a massive impact over time.

✓? Your future health depends on today's choices.

? Now, it's time to act. ?

Mental Health & Emotional Traps: The Lies We Tell Ourselves

CHAPTER SIX

Understanding Mental Traps and Self-Deception

1. Introduction: The Invisible Prison of Our Mind

Our minds are powerful tools that shape our perception of reality. They can be our greatest allies or our most deceptive enemies. The stories we tell ourselves—whether consciously or unconsciously—govern our actions, decisions, and ultimately, our fate.

Consider this: Have you ever told yourself you weren't good enough for an opportunity, only to later realize you were more than capable? Or have you justified staying in a toxic situation, convincing yourself that things weren't "that bad"? These are classic examples of mental traps—patterns of thinking that distort our perception, keeping us stuck in cycles of self-doubt, avoidance, or fear.

We lie to ourselves more than we realize. We justify poor decisions, rationalize our failures, and cling to false beliefs simply because they feel safe. But these deceptions come at a cost—they prevent growth, stall success, and make happiness feel perpetually out of reach.

This section explores why we fall into these mental traps, how our brains deceive us, and what we can do to break free from them.

2. Why Do We Lie to Ourselves? The Science Behind Self-Deception

<u>The Brain's Need for Consistency</u>

Our minds crave consistency and coherence. When faced with contradictions between our beliefs and our actions, our brain works overtime to restore balance, often by distorting reality. This phenomenon, known as cognitive dissonance, explains why we justify bad habits, unhealthy relationships, or poor financial decisions rather than confront the truth.

For example, a smoker might think, "I know smoking is bad for me, but I've been doing it for years, and I'm still fine." Rather than quitting, they adjust their belief to reduce discomfort.

<u>The Role of Defense Mechanisms</u>

Our minds use defense mechanisms to protect us from emotional pain. While these mechanisms serve a purpose, they often lead to self-deception. Here are the most common ones:

Denial – Refusing to accept reality, e.g., ignoring clear signs of an unhealthy relationship.

Rationalization – Justifying poor choices, e.g., "I didn't get that job because the hiring process was unfair."

Projection – Attributing our own negative traits to others, e.g., calling someone else arrogant when we struggle with confidence.

<u>How These Lies Keep Us Stuck</u>

The problem with self-deception is that it reinforces stagnation. The longer we tell ourselves the same false narratives, the harder they become to break. Our comfort zones become prisons, keeping us from realizing our full potential.

3. The Most Common Cognitive Biases That Trap Us

Mental traps are often reinforced by cognitive biases, or systematic errors in thinking that affect our decisions and judgments. Here are some of the most common ones:

<u>1. Confirmation Bias</u>

We seek out information that confirms what we already believe while ignoring contradictory evidence.

Example: A person convinced that all relationships are destined to fail will focus only on negative stories while disregarding successful ones.

<u>2. Self-Serving Bias</u>

We attribute our successes to personal ability but blame failures on external factors.

Example: "I got promoted because I'm talented" vs. "I didn't get the job because the interviewer was biased."

<u>3. Hindsight Bias</u>

We believe, after an event has occurred, that we "knew it all along."

Example: After losing money in a bad investment, someone might say, "I always knew it was risky."

<u>4. Overconfidence Bias</u>

We overestimate our knowledge and abilities, leading to risky decisions.

Example: Someone who has watched a few investment videos on YouTube assumes they can successfully predict stock market trends.

<u>5. Negativity Bias</u>

We focus more on negative experiences than positive ones, which distorts our view of reality.

Example: A person who has experienced one bad relationship assumes all future relationships will also fail.

4. How Mental Traps Shape Our Reality

<u>The Stories We Tell Ourselves Become Our Truth</u>

Our beliefs, whether true or false, shape our behavior. If you repeatedly tell yourself, "I'm bad with money," you will subconsciously make choices that reinforce this belief. Your thoughts create a self-fulfilling prophecy.

<u>The Comfort Zone and the Fear of Change</u>

Mental traps often keep us stuck in our comfort zones. While the familiar feels safe, it also limits growth.

Example: Someone who believes they "aren't good at public speaking" avoids opportunities to develop the skill, reinforcing their fear.

<u>Why We Resist Facing the Truth</u>

Facing reality requires effort, change, and sometimes pain. It's easier to blame external factors or tell ourselves comforting lies than to accept the responsibility of making changes.

Society also reinforces certain mental traps:

Toxic positivity – The idea that we should always "stay positive" can prevent us from acknowledging real problems.

Hustle culture – The belief that working constantly equals success leads to burnout and stress.

5. Breaking Free from Mental Traps: A First Step

<u>Awareness is the First Step</u>

The first step to escaping mental traps is recognizing them.

Start by identifying recurring negative thoughts.

Ask: "Where did this belief come from? Is it really true?"

<u>Challenging False Narratives</u>

One of the most powerful tools for change is cognitive reframing—the process of shifting our perspective.

Instead of "I'm terrible at networking," try "I haven't practiced networking yet, but I can learn."

<u>The Power of Perspective Shifts</u>

Sometimes, the key to breaking free from mental traps is seeking outside perspectives—whether through therapy, coaching, or honest conversations.

Therapists help us challenge distorted thinking patterns.

Mentors provide guidance to break out of limiting beliefs.

<u>Journaling helps us reflect and question our assumptions.</u>

1. Why Do We Deceive Ourselves?

Self-deception is a fundamental aspect of human psychology. It allows us to justify our actions, maintain a sense of stability, and protect ourselves from uncomfortable truths. While it serves as a defense mechanism, it can also hinder personal growth, damage relationships, and lead to poor decision-making.

Cognitive Dissonance: The Need for Mental Consistency

Cognitive dissonance occurs when there is a conflict between our beliefs and actions. Our brain attempts to resolve this inconsistency by altering our perceptions rather than changing our behavior. For example:

A smoker who knows smoking is harmful might rationalize their habit by saying, "It helps me relax."

Someone staying in a toxic relationship might convince themselves, "They will change eventually."

Emotional Avoidance: Shielding Ourselves from Pain

We often deceive ourselves to escape discomfort. Facing reality may require admitting failures, taking responsibility, or making difficult changes. This avoidance manifests in different ways:

Ignoring financial problems by refusing to check bank statements.

Denying the need for therapy despite ongoing emotional distress.

Social Conditioning and Self-Deception

Society reinforces certain false beliefs. Cultural norms, family expectations, and peer pressure often shape our self-deceptions. Examples include:

"I must always be strong; showing emotions is weakness."

"Success is measured only by wealth and status."

2. The Neuroscience Behind Self-Deception

How the Brain Sustains False Beliefs

Multiple brain regions contribute to self-deception:

Prefrontal Cortex: Responsible for rationalizing and maintaining self-justifications.

Amygdala: Processes emotions and reinforces avoidance of uncomfortable truths.

Dopamine System: Rewards us for beliefs that align with comfort and short-term pleasure.

Neuroscientific research suggests that self-deception is an adaptive function, helping humans navigate complex social structures. However, unchecked self-deception can create long-term psychological and emotional harm.

3. Types of Self-Deception

1. The Justification Trap

Fabricating reasons to validate actions and avoid accountability.

Example: "I didn't exercise today because I had a stressful day at work."

2. False Optimism

Overestimating positive outcomes while ignoring reality.

Example: A chronic procrastinator believing they will finish a project last minute without preparation.

3. The Illusion of Control

Believing we have more influence over situations than we actually do.

Example: A gambler thinking they can "control" their luck.

4. Selective Memory

Remembering successes more vividly than failures.

Example: Recalling only the positive aspects of a past relationship while ignoring the toxicity.

5. The "I'll Change Tomorrow" Lie

A form of procrastination disguised as self-improvement.

Example: "I'll start eating healthy next Monday."

4. The Psychological Cost of Self-Deception

Emotional Exhaustion

Maintaining false beliefs requires mental energy, leading to stress and burnout.

Poor Decision-Making

Ignoring facts and justifying poor choices results in repeated mistakes and setbacks.

Strained Relationships

Self-deception can cause misunderstandings, unmet expectations, and avoidance of accountability.

Personal Stagnation

When we deceive ourselves, we resist change and limit our potential for growth.

5. Strategies to Overcome Self-Deception

1. Developing Self-Awareness

Journaling: Writing down thoughts and emotions can reveal inconsistencies in our beliefs.

Mindfulness: Helps recognize avoidance behaviors and accept uncomfortable truths.

Asking Hard Questions: "Am I making excuses, or is this truly valid?"

2. Reframing Thought Patterns

Challenging negative beliefs: Replace "I always fail" with "I've faced setbacks, but I've also succeeded."

3. Seeking External Perspectives

Therapy or coaching can help uncover deep-seated self-deceptions.

Feedback from trusted friends or mentors can provide objective insights.

4. Accepting Discomfort as a Sign of Growth

Growth requires facing difficult truths rather than hiding behind self-deception.

Viewing discomfort as a sign of personal development rather than a threat.

5. Moving Forward: Embracing Truth and Growth

<u>Truths to Embrace:</u>

You are more resilient than you think.

Progress is always possible, no matter where you start.

Happiness is not a future event; it's created in the present.

You deserve good things, and you have the power to claim them.

Breaking free from self-deception is an ongoing process, but every step toward truth is a step toward a better, more fulfilling life.

CHAPTER SEVEN

THE LIES WE TELL OURSELVES

1. Introduction: The Comfort of Deception

We lie to ourselves more often than we realize. Sometimes, these lies are harmless, like telling ourselves we'll start eating healthy "tomorrow." Other times, they keep us trapped in cycles of self-doubt, avoidance, and unfulfilled potential. The lies we tell ourselves shape our decisions, relationships, and mental well-being.

This section explores some of the most common self-deceptions, why we hold onto them, and how we can break free.

2. The Most Common Lies We Tell Ourselves

<u>1. "I Am Not Good Enough"</u>

The Root of the Lie: Often stems from childhood conditioning, comparisons, or past failures.

The Impact: Leads to low self-esteem, fear of failure, and avoiding opportunities.

Breaking Free: Challenge negative self-talk, list past achievements, and take small risks to build confidence.

<u>2. "If I Ignore It, It Will Go Away"</u>

The Root of the Lie: Avoidance coping mechanism to escape uncomfortable situations.

The Impact: Problems (financial, emotional, or health-related) worsen over time.

Breaking Free: Face issues head-on, seek advice, and set action plans for resolution.

<u>3. "I Will Be Happy When..."</u>

The Root of the Lie: Society's conditioning to chase external success for happiness.

The Impact: Creates a cycle of perpetual dissatisfaction, always seeking more.

Breaking Free: Focus on present joys, practice gratitude, and redefine success on your terms.

<u>4. "I Don't Deserve Good Things"</u>

The Root of the Lie: Deep-seated guilt, unworthiness, or past mistakes.

The Impact: Leads to self-sabotage and settling for less than we deserve.

Breaking Free: Identify the source of this belief, practice self-compassion, and allow yourself to accept joy.

<u>5. "They Must Be Right About Me"</u>

The Root of the Lie: External validation and fear of judgment.

The Impact: Loss of personal identity and living based on others' expectations.

Breaking Free: Differentiate constructive feedback from criticism, trust your intuition, and define yourself on your terms.

<u>6. "It's Too Late to Change"</u>

The Root of the Lie: Fear of failure, societal expectations about age or time limits.

The Impact: Leads to stagnation, regret, and unfulfilled dreams.

Breaking Free: Embrace lifelong learning, seek new experiences, and recognize that change is always possible.

3. The Psychological Cost of Self-Deception

Emotional Drain: Constantly believing lies requires mental effort, leading to stress and exhaustion.

Missed Opportunities: Avoiding risks and chances due to false beliefs results in unrealized potential.

Strained Relationships: Self-deception can cause misunderstandings, unspoken needs, and conflicts.

Decision Paralysis: Holding onto limiting beliefs prevents us from making confident choices.

4. How to Recognize and Challenge These Lies

<u>1. Self-Awareness: Identifying Personal Mental Lies</u>

Keep a thought journal to track recurring negative thoughts.

Ask, "Is this belief based on facts or assumptions?"

Seek feedback from close friends or mentors who provide honest perspectives.

<u>2. Reframing Thoughts with Truth</u>
Instead of "I'm not good enough," say "I am capable, and I am learning."
Replace "It's too late" with "I can start now and make progress."
<u>3. Seeking Help and Guidance</u>
Therapy or coaching can help uncover deep-rooted false beliefs.
Books and self-development resources offer new perspectives.
Surround yourself with people who challenge and uplift you.

5. Moving Forward: Embracing Truth and Growth

The Truths to Embrace:

You are more resilient than you think.

Progress is always possible, no matter where you start.

Happiness is not a future event; it's created in the present.

You deserve good things, and you have the power to claim them.

Breaking free from self-deception is an ongoing process, but every step towards truth is a step towards a better, more fulfilling life.

What's Next? In the following section, we'll explore how emotional traps reinforce these mental lies and how to dismantle them effectively.

CHAPTER EIGHT

EMOTIONAL TRAPS AND THEIR CONSEQUENCES

1. Introduction: The Invisible Chains of Emotional Traps

Emotional traps are deceptive patterns of thinking and behavior that keep us stuck in cycles of negativity, self-doubt, and fear. They often masquerade as protective mechanisms, but in reality, they limit our growth, damage relationships, and hinder success. Understanding these traps and their consequences is the first step in breaking free from them.

This section explores the most common emotional traps, their psychological impact, and strategies to overcome them.

2. Common Emotional Traps

<u>1. The Overthinking Trap</u>

What It Is: An endless cycle of analyzing, second-guessing, and worrying about decisions or situations.

Why It Happens: Fear of making mistakes, perfectionism, or lack of confidence.

Consequences: Decision paralysis, anxiety, and missed opportunities.

Breaking Free: Practice mindfulness, set decision deadlines, and accept that uncertainty is a part of life.

<u>2. The Fear of Failure Trap</u>

What It Is: Avoiding risks or new challenges due to the fear of failing.

Why It Happens: Past failures, societal expectations, or self-imposed pressure.

Consequences: Stagnation, unfulfilled potential, and regret.

Breaking Free: Reframe failure as a learning experience, take small calculated risks, and focus on progress over perfection.

<u>3. The Perfectionism Trap</u>

What It Is: The relentless pursuit of flawlessness, often leading to self-criticism and stress.

Why It Happens: Fear of judgment, unrealistic standards, or childhood conditioning.

Consequences: Procrastination, burnout, and dissatisfaction.

Breaking Free: Embrace imperfection, set realistic goals, and celebrate small achievements.

<u>4. The Comparison Trap</u>

What It Is: Measuring one's success, happiness, or worth against others.

Why It Happens: Social media influence, societal pressure, or low self-esteem.

Consequences: Decreased self-worth, resentment, and distraction from personal goals.

Breaking Free: Focus on self-growth, practice gratitude, and limit social media exposure.

<u>5. The Guilt & Shame Trap</u>

What It Is: Holding onto past mistakes or feeling unworthy due to societal or personal expectations.

Why It Happens: Moral conditioning, harsh self-judgment, or unresolved trauma.

Consequences: Emotional paralysis, self-sabotage, and mental health struggles.

Breaking Free: Practice self-forgiveness, seek therapy if needed, and differentiate between guilt (learning tool) and shame (destructive emotion).

<u>6. The People-Pleasing Trap</u>

What It Is: Constantly prioritizing others' needs and approval over one's own.

Why It Happens: Fear of rejection, need for validation, or lack of boundaries.

Consequences: Loss of identity, resentment, and emotional exhaustion.

Breaking Free: Set boundaries, learn to say no, and prioritize self-care.

<u>7. The Comfort Zone Trap</u>

What It Is: Staying in familiar but limiting situations to avoid discomfort.

Why It Happens: Fear of uncertainty, past trauma, or lack of confidence.

Consequences: Missed growth opportunities, stagnation, and regret.

Breaking Free: Take small steps outside the comfort zone, embrace challenges, and cultivate a growth mindset.

3. The Psychological and Emotional Consequences of These Traps

<u>1. Increased Anxiety and Stress</u>

Emotional traps keep the brain in a constant state of worry and tension.

Leads to heightened cortisol levels, affecting overall health.

<u>2. Low Self-Worth and Confidence</u>

Repeated self-doubt reinforces negative self-perceptions.

Limits the ability to take on new challenges or trust oneself.

<u>3. Strained Relationships</u>

Emotional traps, like people-pleasing and guilt, create resentment in relationships.

Lack of authenticity in relationships leads to unfulfilled connections.

<u>4. Stagnation and Regret</u>

Avoiding risks or staying in toxic situations leads to missed opportunities.

The longer one remains in these traps, the harder it becomes to break free.

<u>5. Impact on Mental and Physical Health</u>

Chronic stress, self-doubt, and emotional suppression can lead to depression, anxiety disorders, and physical illnesses.

Emotional well-being is directly linked to physical health.

4. Strategies to Overcome Emotional Traps

<u>1. Self-Awareness and Mindfulness</u>

Recognizing patterns of emotional traps is the first step to change.

Journaling, meditation, and therapy can help uncover deep-seated issues.

<u>2. Cognitive Reframing</u>

Challenge irrational thoughts and replace them with constructive beliefs.

Example: Instead of "I must be perfect," say "I strive to do my best, but imperfection is part of being human."

<u>3. Setting Boundaries</u>

Prioritize personal well-being over external validation.

Practice assertiveness in relationships and commitments.

<u>4. Taking Small, Purposeful Risks</u>

Growth happens outside the comfort zone.

Start with manageable challenges to build confidence and resilience.

<u>5. Seeking Support and Guidance</u>

Therapy, support groups, or mentors can provide perspective and encouragement.

Sharing struggles with trusted individuals helps lessen the emotional burden.

5. Moving Forward: Choosing Growth Over Emotional Traps

Escaping emotional traps requires conscious effort, patience, and self-compassion. The key is to recognize the patterns, challenge limiting beliefs, and take deliberate steps toward personal freedom.

Truths to Embrace:

Growth comes with discomfort, but it leads to fulfillment.

You are worthy, even if you make mistakes.

Comparison steals joy—focus on your unique journey.

Small steps outside your comfort zone lead to great transformations.

Breaking free from emotional traps is not an overnight process, but with persistence and self-awareness, true personal freedom is achievable.

CHAPTER NINE

Healing, Mental Health, and Rewriting Your Narrative

1. Introduction: The Power of Healing and Self-Renewal

Healing is an ongoing journey, not a destination. Our mental health plays a crucial role in shaping our identity, decisions, and future. When we carry past traumas, limiting beliefs, and emotional baggage, they distort our perception of ourselves and the world. The good news is that we have the power to rewrite our narrative, heal from our wounds, and take control of our mental well-being.

This section explores the foundations of mental health, strategies for healing, and actionable steps to reshape our personal narratives for a healthier, more fulfilling life.

2. Understanding Mental Health and Emotional Healing

<u>1. The Connection Between Mental Health and Personal Growth</u>

Mental health is the foundation for self-awareness, decision-making, and emotional resilience.

Healing begins when we acknowledge the impact of our thoughts, emotions, and behaviors.

<u>2. Common Barriers to Healing</u>

Denial: Refusing to confront painful past experiences.

Guilt and Shame: Carrying self-blame for past mistakes or situations beyond our control.

Fear of Vulnerability: Avoiding emotional expression due to fear of judgment or rejection.

Negative Self-Talk: Internalizing toxic narratives that reinforce self-doubt and unworthiness.

3. The Science Behind Emotional Healing

The brain's neuroplasticity allows us to rewire negative thought patterns and create healthier coping mechanisms.

Practicing mindfulness and self-compassion activates the parasympathetic nervous system, reducing stress and promoting healing.

Building emotional intelligence helps process past wounds and navigate life with greater ease.

3. Steps to Healing and Mental Well-Being

1. Acknowledging and Accepting Your Past

Healing starts with acknowledging past wounds rather than suppressing them.

Acceptance does not mean approval; it means making peace with what has happened.

Journaling or therapy can help bring suppressed emotions to the surface.

2. Releasing Toxic Emotional Baggage

Forgiveness is a tool for liberation, not for excusing harm.

Letting go of resentment and self-blame can create space for new perspectives.

Engage in emotional release techniques like meditation, deep breathing, or creative expression.

3. Establishing Healthier Thought Patterns

Replace negative self-talk with affirmations and constructive self-reflection.

Challenge irrational fears and catastrophic thinking.

Reframe failures as learning opportunities rather than personal shortcomings.

4. Cultivating Mindfulness and Emotional Resilience

Mindfulness practices like meditation, gratitude exercises, and breathing techniques help regulate emotions.

Emotional resilience is built through self-awareness, adaptability, and problem-solving skills.

Learning to sit with discomfort and uncertainty is crucial for long-term mental well-being.

4. Rewriting Your Narrative: A New Chapter of Self-Empowerment

<u>1. Identifying and Dismantling Old Narratives</u>

What stories do you tell yourself about who you are?

Identify self-limiting beliefs that stem from past experiences, social conditioning, or internalized criticism.

Question their validity: Are these beliefs helping or hindering your growth?

<u>2. Crafting a New Story Based on Self-Compassion and Possibility</u>

Replace "I am not enough" with "I am learning and growing."

Redefine success and happiness on your own terms.

Set intentions aligned with your values and aspirations.

<u>3. Taking Action: Living Out Your New Narrative</u>

Small, consistent actions reinforce a new self-image.

Surround yourself with people who support and uplift you.

Invest in self-care, education, and experiences that align with your evolving identity.

5. Moving Forward: Embracing Healing as a Lifelong Process

Healing is not linear; it is a continuous process of learning, unlearning, and evolving. By taking control of our mental health and rewriting our personal narratives, we empower ourselves to live with greater peace, purpose, and authenticity.

Key Truths to Embrace:

Healing is a journey, not a destination.

You are not defined by your past.

Growth and self-compassion are choices you can make every day.

Your story is yours to write—choose one that empowers you.

Every step toward healing and self-discovery brings you closer to the person you are meant to be.

CHAPTER TEN

THE TRUTHS WE MUST EMBRACE

1. Introduction: Embracing Reality for Personal Growth

The path to personal transformation is not just about unlearning falsehoods but also about embracing fundamental truths that shape our resilience, confidence, and overall well-being. These truths are often difficult to accept because they challenge our comfort zones and force us to confront deep-seated fears and limiting beliefs. However, only by acknowledging and internalizing these realities can we truly grow and live authentically.

This section explores key truths we must embrace to achieve lasting fulfillment and peace.

Truth #1: Growth Requires Discomfort

True growth does not come from staying in our comfort zones but from facing challenges head-on.

Fear, failure, and uncertainty are not signs to retreat; they are necessary experiences for transformation.

Embracing discomfort means being open to learning, making mistakes, and adapting.

Practical steps: Engage in activities that push your limits, seek constructive feedback, and develop resilience in the face of adversity.

Truth #2: You Are Not Your Past

Our past experiences shape us, but they do not define us.

Holding onto past mistakes, regrets, or traumas prevents us from moving forward.

Healing and growth come from recognizing that change is always possible.

Practical steps: Practice self-forgiveness, reframe past experiences as lessons, and focus on present opportunities.

Truth #3: Happiness Comes from Within

External achievements, relationships, and possessions may bring temporary happiness, but true contentment is cultivated internally.

Relying on external validation makes happiness fragile and dependent on circumstances beyond our control.

Cultivating inner peace through gratitude, mindfulness, and self-acceptance leads to lasting fulfillment.

Practical steps: Develop daily gratitude practices, limit dependence on social approval, and engage in activities that bring intrinsic joy.

Truth #4: Failure Is an Essential Part of Success

Every successful individual has faced setbacks and failures.

Viewing failure as an end point limits growth, whereas seeing it as a learning opportunity propels us forward.

Practical steps: Reframe failures as valuable lessons, adopt a growth mindset, and focus on persistence over perfection.

Truth #5: You Cannot Control Everything

Obsessing over things beyond our control leads to unnecessary stress and anxiety.

Learning to let go and focus on what we can influence empowers us.

Practical steps: Identify areas within your control, practice acceptance of uncertainty, and cultivate adaptability.

Truth #6: Self-Worth Is Not Conditional

Your value is not determined by achievements, relationships, or societal standards.

Embracing self-worth means accepting yourself as you are while striving for growth.

Practical steps: Challenge negative self-talk, practice self-compassion, and surround yourself with supportive influences.

Truth #7: Change Is Always Possible

No matter how long you have believed in a limiting story, change is within reach.

Small, consistent efforts lead to profound transformations over time.

Practical steps: Set realistic goals, track progress, and remain open to new perspectives.

2. Moving Forward: Living with Intention and Authenticity

Embracing these truths is not a one-time realization but a continuous journey. The more we align our thoughts and actions with these realities, the more we empower ourselves to live with authenticity, resilience, and fulfillment.

<u>Key Takeaways:</u>

Growth is uncomfortable but necessary.

The past does not define your future.

Happiness is cultivated from within.

Failure is a stepping stone to success.

Focus on what you can control and release the rest.

Your worth is inherent, not conditional.

Change is always possible.

By internalizing these truths, we step into a life of clarity, strength, and purpose—one where we no longer resist reality but embrace it as a foundation for limitless possibilities.

Love & Romantic Relationships: When Affection Turns into a Ponzi Scheme

CHAPTER ELEVEN

THE ILLUSION OF EVERLASTING LOVE – SETTING THE STAGE

1.1 The Promise of Love: A Fairy Tale Beginning

From the moment we are born, we are sold an idea of love that is intoxicatingly beautiful. It is a concept wrapped in grand gestures, everlasting passion, and the promise of unwavering companionship. Fairytales, novels, movies, and even social media reinforce this narrative, portraying love as the ultimate achievement in life.

Love stories in Hollywood and Bollywood follow a predictable pattern: two people meet under extraordinary circumstances, experience a whirlwind romance, overcome dramatic obstacles, and finally, live happily ever after. The story conveniently ends right before reality sets in. There's no sequel depicting the emotional exhaustion of constant compromise, the slow erosion of excitement, or the struggles of sustaining affection in the long run.

Much like an investor looking for a get-rich-quick scheme, people enter relationships with the expectation of guaranteed returns—eternal happiness, emotional fulfillment, and mutual support. But what happens when these returns start diminishing? When the promise of lifelong affection turns out to be a myth, the illusion begins to crack.

1.2 Love Bombing: The Grand Entry of the Scheme

Every Ponzi scheme begins with a charismatic recruiter promising extraordinary benefits. In love, this role is played by the partner who showers their significant other with intense affection, attention, and grand declarations of devotion. This psychological manipulation tactic is known as love bombing, and it's the emotional equivalent of an investment scam.

In the early stages of a Ponzi scheme, new investors are lured in with promises of massive profits. They are given returns—not from real gains but from money collected from newer investors. Similarly, in relationships, the beginning often feels too good to be true.

"You're the most amazing person I've ever met."

"I've never felt this way before."

"I can't imagine my life without you."

These words, paired with excessive gifts, constant messages, and undivided attention, create an artificial sense of security. The recipient of such affection feels lucky, chosen, and special—just like an early investor believing they've found a rare financial opportunity.

However, just as Ponzi schemes are unsustainable, so is this level of overwhelming affection. It is a front-loaded investment meant to create dependency. The moment the victim is emotionally invested, the real scheme begins.

1.3 The Early Investors vs. Late Investors in Relationships

The initial excitement in a romantic relationship is akin to the early stages of a booming Ponzi scheme. The first investors (or in this case, the first phase of the relationship) receive the highest returns. They get the attention, the romantic gestures, and the emotional high that makes love feel like a dream.

But what happens when more time passes? Just as later investors in a Ponzi scheme receive fewer and fewer benefits before the scheme eventually collapses, late-stage partners in a relationship notice diminishing returns.

The good morning and goodnight texts become infrequent.

The spontaneous gifts and surprises stop.

The long, deep conversations turn into brief, distracted exchanges.

At first, the recipient of these diminishing returns blames external factors—work stress, personal issues, or routine fatigue. But just like a Ponzi scheme running out of new investors, the reality is simple: the initial stage was unsustainable, designed only to lure the partner in.

Love, in its healthiest form, should be like a long-term investment with steady, gradual returns rather than a high-risk scheme with an inevitable crash. However, most people are conditioned to expect love to function like a Ponzi scheme—where the early investors (new relationships) get everything, while long-term relationships often result in emotional bankruptcy.

Conclusion: The Illusion That Keeps the Scheme Running

If we break it down, love is often sold like a financial scam. Society conditions us to chase it, invest in it blindly, and ignore the warning signs that something isn't right. But unlike financial fraud, emotional Ponzi schemes can be even more damaging. They leave scars of self-doubt, trust issues, and emotional exhaustion.

The key to avoiding this illusion is awareness—understanding that love should not be a manipulation tactic, a dependency trap, or a transaction. In the next part, we will explore how relationships, much like business models, often operate on unfair structures where one person benefits at the expense of the other.

CHAPTER TWELVE

The Recruitment Phase – Love as a Business Model

2.1 The ROI (Return on Investment) Fallacy

In finance, an investor puts money into a project expecting future profits. In relationships, people invest time, emotions, and effort with the expectation of love, loyalty, and security. But just like in a Ponzi scheme, the promised returns are often exaggerated, and many people end up with far less than they invested.

A fundamental problem with love is that people tend to overestimate the stability of their emotional investment. The concept of sunk cost fallacy—where individuals continue investing in something simply because they have already put so much into it—applies heavily to relationships.

Consider these common thoughts:

"We've been together for five years; I can't just walk away now."

"I've done so much for them; I just need to try harder."

"Maybe if I wait a little longer, things will go back to how they were in the beginning."

These thoughts mirror those of a financial scam victim who refuses to withdraw their money because they hope the scheme will eventually work. They ignore the warning signs, delay making hard decisions, and continue investing in something that is already collapsing.

The emotional ROI fallacy blinds people to the truth: a relationship's past success does not guarantee future returns. Unlike a financial investment, there are no guaranteed dividends in love.

2.2 The High-Value Partner as the Mastermind

Every Ponzi scheme has a charismatic leader who appears to have the secret formula for success. In relationships, this role is often played by the high-value partner—someone who creates the illusion that they are a rare catch, forcing the other person to prove their worth.

This partner may:

Be selectively affectionate, offering love only when they need something in return.

Use future faking, making big promises about marriage, kids, or shared dreams to keep the other person emotionally hooked.

Manipulate using scarcity tactics, implying that the partner isn't good enough and must "work harder" to earn their affection.

One classic example of this is love fraud, where con artists intentionally enter relationships to exploit their partner financially or emotionally. Stories of men and women who have emptied their savings for a deceitful lover are disturbingly common. But financial fraud isn't the only form of abuse—emotional fraud is equally damaging, leaving victims feeling used and discarded.

Gaslighting is another critical manipulation tactic in these scenarios. The manipulator makes their partner doubt their own judgment, making them more reliant on the relationship for emotional stability. Statements like:

"You're overreacting, I never said that."

"If you really loved me, you wouldn't question me."

"You're imagining things."

...are all psychological tricks to keep control over the "investor" in the relationship.

2.3 Relationship Pyramids: Who's on Top?

Every Ponzi scheme is structured as a pyramid: those at the top benefit, while those at the bottom suffer. Relationships often operate in the same way, though less obviously.

Some partners function as investors, constantly giving time, energy, and sacrifices. Others function as consumers, benefiting without reciprocating. Over time, a power imbalance develops, where one person does all the emotional labor while the other enjoys the returns.

<u>Common patterns in relationship pyramids include:</u>

The Constant Giver vs. The Taker – One partner is always planning dates, making sacrifices, or fixing issues, while the other just enjoys the benefits.

The Validation Seeker vs. The Dismissive Partner – One partner is always chasing love and approval, while the other remains emotionally distant.

The Caregiver vs. The Dependent – One partner acts as a therapist, supporting the other emotionally, while their own needs are ignored.

Just like a Ponzi scheme collapses when new investors stop joining, relationships break down when the giver realizes they are in a one-sided transaction. The moment they stop investing, the entire dynamic falls apart.

Conclusion: Love as an Unsustainable Business Model

A good business model is sustainable, ensuring long-term balance between effort and reward. But in many relationships, one partner continuously overinvests while the other reaps the benefits. This creates a toxic cycle that eventually leads to collapse.

To break free from this system, individuals must audit their emotional investments just as they would audit their finances. They must ask themselves:

Am I the only one putting effort into this relationship?

Does my partner reciprocate, or do they just take?

If I stopped investing tomorrow, would the relationship still survive?

Understanding these dynamics is the first step toward healthier relationships—ones based on mutual effort rather than manipulation and deceit.

CHAPTER THIRTEEN

THE COLLAPSE – WHEN THE LOVE FUNDS DRY UP

3.1 The First Red Flags

In the early stages of a Ponzi scheme, everything looks promising. Investors see initial gains and are convinced they've made the right choice. However, beneath the surface, the scheme is fragile—it can only survive as long as new investments keep coming. The same applies to romantic relationships built on emotional deception.

Every unsustainable relationship eventually starts showing cracks. These are the first red flags, warning signs that the affection, attention, and emotional security once promised are running dry.

<u>Common Early Red Flags in a Relationship Ponzi Scheme:</u>

The Sudden Withdrawal of Affection

What once felt like an endless supply of love and validation starts dwindling.

The affectionate texts become infrequent.

The time spent together starts to feel transactional rather than meaningful.

Excuses and Justifications

"I've just been so busy lately."

"Things are really stressful at work."

"I just need some space right now."

While these might seem reasonable, they often serve as subtle ways to withdraw from the relationship without dirrect confrontation.

Inconsistent Behavior

One day, they're full of warmth and love; the next, they're cold and distant.

This emotional rollercoaster keeps the victim emotionally invested, hoping that the good days will return.

Blame-Shifting

The partner no longer takes responsibility for the decline in affection.

"You're too needy."

"You're imagining things."

"You've changed."

The blame is placed on the investor, making them work harder to win back the love they're losing.

The victim, much like an investor in a collapsing Ponzi scheme, refuses to accept the truth. They hold onto the initial promises, hoping the affection will return. But the scheme is already falling apart.

3.2 Emotional Bankruptcy – When the Scheme Crashes

A Ponzi scheme eventually collapses when new investors stop coming in and the system can no longer sustain itself. In relationships, this moment comes when the emotional "investor" finally realizes they are running on empty.

<u>The Emotional Bankruptcy Phase</u>

The investor feels exhausted, constantly giving but receiving nothing in return.

They experience self-doubt, wondering if they did something wrong.

Feelings of resentment and frustration replace the love they once felt.

Anxiety builds, as they realize their partner is no longer emotionally available.

This is the breaking point—the realization that the love they invested in was never real.

<u>The Gradual Fade</u>

The partner slowly drifts away, making fewer efforts, initiating fewer conversations, and letting the connection die naturally.

The investor is left wondering what they did wrong and may even chase after the partner, trying to reignite the lost spark.

<u>The Abrupt Disappearance</u>

Also known as ghosting, the partner suddenly disappears with no explanation.

One day, everything seems fine, and the next, they're gone—blocking calls, ignoring messages, and moving on as if the relationship never existed.

This is one of the most painful ways the collapse happens, as it leaves the victim without closure.

<u>The Cruel Exit Strategy</u>

Instead of fading away, the manipulative partner blames the victim for everything.

"You're too demanding."

"I don't feel the same way anymore."

"I need to focus on myself."

These statements are designed to make the victim feel guilty and responsible for the breakup, despite the fact that they were the ones being exploited.

<u>The Quick Replacement</u>

The emotional con artist moves on instantly, finding a new "investor" to supply the affection and validation they need.

The victim is left confused and heartbroken, wondering how someone who claimed to love them could move on so quickly.

At this stage, the truth is undeniable—the relationship was a Ponzi scheme, and the investor has lost everything.

3.3 The Exit Strategy: How Con Artists Escape

Just as financial fraudsters flee when their scheme collapses, emotional manipulators have their own exit strategies to avoid responsibility.

<u>Common Escape Tactics of Emotional Con Artists:</u>

Disappearing Without a Trace

Completely cutting off all contact, ignoring messages, and pretending the relationship never existed.

This is a tactic to avoid difficult conversations and accountability.

Creating a False Narrative

Blaming the victim for the relationship's failure.

Telling mutual friends that they were the ones who wanted to leave.

Manipulating others into believing the victim was too demanding or too emotional.

Jumping Into a New Relationship

Quickly finding a new partner to distract from their own issues.

This serves two purposes:

It validates that they are still desirable.

It prevents them from having to process their own emotions.

Offering False Hope

Keeping the victim on standby with occasional texts like:

"I miss you."

"Maybe we just need some time apart."

"Let's see where life takes us."

This is meant to keep the victim emotionally invested, preventing them from fully moving on.

These tactics show that the manipulative partner was never emotionally invested in the relationship—they were simply benefiting from the affection and effort their partner provided.

Conclusion: The Aftermath of an Emotional Ponzi Scheme

When a Ponzi scheme collapses, investors are left devastated, often facing financial ruin. In a collapsed relationship Ponzi scheme, the emotional investor is left feeling:

Betrayed: Realizing they were used for their affection, time, or resources.

Confused: Struggling to understand why the relationship ended the way it did.

Self-Doubting: Wondering if they were the problem all along.

Exhausted: Emotionally drained from investing so much without returns.

The biggest challenge post-collapse is accepting the reality—that the love they believed in was a lie.

The healing process is long and painful, but it begins with understanding what happened and learning to rebuild self-worth. In the next part, we will explore how to audit your love life and protect yourself from future emotional Ponzi schemes.

LESSONS FROM A FRAUD EXAMINER – HOW TO AUDIT YOUR LOVE LIFE

Fraud examiners are trained to spot deception, identify red flags, and investigate financial inconsistencies. But what if we applied the same principles to relationships? What if we audited our love life the way a fraud examiner audits financial records?

When it comes to love, people tend to ignore warning signs, overlook inconsistencies, and blindly trust based on emotions. However, much like financial fraud, relationship scams leave victims emotionally bankrupt and filled with regret. The key to preventing emotional fraud is due diligence—learning how to analyze relationships with a clear, investigative mindset.

4.1 Due Diligence Before Investing in Love

Before making any major financial investment, a fraud examiner conducts due diligence—analyzing financial statements, checking for irregularities, and verifying information. The same principle should apply before fully investing in a relationship.

How to Perform Due Diligence in Relationships:

<u>1. Verify Before You Trust</u>

Just as you wouldn't trust a company without checking its financial reports, don't blindly trust someone based on words alone.

Pay attention to actions over promises—does their behavior align with what they say?

Observe how they treat others, not just how they treat you in the beginning.

2. Look for "Too Good to Be True" Red Flags

In fraud cases, if an investment sounds too good to be true, it usually is.

In love, if someone seems too perfect, showers you with excessive affection too soon, or makes grand promises early on, be cautious.

Healthy relationships take time to build; instant chemistry is often a manipulation tactic.

3. Investigate Their Relationship History

In finance, a company's past performance provides insight into future risks.

In relationships, a person's history of relationships and breakups can reveal patterns.

Questions to ask:

How do they talk about their exes?

Do they take responsibility for past failures, or do they always blame others?

Have they been in long-term, stable relationships before?

4. Observe Their Financial and Emotional Stability

Fraudsters often live beyond their means, promising wealth but having no real assets.

Emotional manipulators often promise deep love and security but lack the emotional maturity to sustain it.

If someone has a history of unstable relationships, dramatic breakups, or financial irresponsibility, it's a warning sign.

4.2 Diversifying Your Emotional Portfolio

In investing, putting all your money into one stock is a high-risk move. Similarly, placing all your emotional well-being into one relationship can be dangerous.

How to Emotionally Diversify:

1. Maintain Your Own Identity

Fraud victims often become financially dependent on the scammer, making it harder to leave.

Similarly, people who lose themselves in relationships struggle to walk away when things turn toxic.

Maintain personal hobbies, friendships, and individual goals outside of the relationship.

<u>2. Avoid Over-Investing Too Soon</u>

Investors start with small investments before committing more funds.

In relationships, pace yourself emotionally—don't give 100% of your heart before seeing if the other person is equally invested.

<u>3. Build Multiple Emotional Support Systems</u>

Just as a diverse investment portfolio protects against financial loss, strong friendships, family bonds, and self-reliance protect against emotional devastation.

Having multiple sources of emotional support prevents one failed relationship from feeling like the end of the world.

4.3 Red Flags and Fraud Prevention Tactics

A fraud examiner is trained to spot red flags—subtle signs of deception in financial statements. Similarly, there are key red flags in relationships that indicate emotional fraud.

<u>Major Red Flags in a Relationship Ponzi Scheme:</u>

Love Bombing: Excessive attention, gifts, and affection too quickly—used to manipulate.

Inconsistencies in Stories: If their words don't match their actions, they may be hiding something.

Lack of Accountability: Always blaming others for their past relationships, never admitting faults.

Fast Escalation: Rushing into commitment, moving in together too soon, or excessive future promises.

Disrespect for Boundaries: Ignoring your comfort levels, pushing you into things you're unsure about.

Emotional Manipulation: Using guilt, fear, or obligation to control you.

Withdrawing Affection Over Time: A pattern where they give less and less once you're emotionally hooked.

Secretive Behavior: Avoiding discussions about past relationships, finances, or personal life.

<u>How to Protect Yourself from Emotional Fraud:</u>

? Set Boundaries Early – Don't let emotions cloud your judgment; establish limits on what you'll accept.

? Conduct "Background Checks" – Without snooping, observe their lifestyle, habits, and how they treat others.

? Pay Attention to Gut Feelings – If something feels off, don't ignore it.

? Watch for Repeated Patterns – If they show behavior that mirrors toxic past relationships, take note.

? Test Reciprocity – Are they investing equally in the relationship, or are you doing all the work?

Conclusion: Love with Due Diligence

In financial fraud cases, victims wish they had seen the warning signs earlier. The same is true for relationships. By auditing our love lives the way fraud examiners audit financial transactions, we can prevent heartbreak, manipulation, and emotional scams.

? Key Takeaways:

✓ Trust should be earned, not given freely.

✓ Pacing a relationship prevents emotional over-investment.

✓ Love should be mutual—imbalances indicate a failing investment.

✓ A strong support system outside of the relationship ensures emotional security.

✓ Red flags should never be ignored; early prevention saves future pain.

By treating love like an intelligent investment, we ensure that our emotional resources are placed in relationships that truly deserve them.

CHAPTER FIFTEEN

REBUILDING AFTER EMOTIONAL FRAUD – FROM VICTIM TO VICTOR

A Ponzi scheme doesn't just take away money; it robs people of their trust, confidence, and sense of security. Similarly, an emotional Ponzi scheme doesn't just end in heartbreak—it leaves victims questioning their self-worth, decision-making, and ability to trust again.

However, just as financial fraud victims can recover by learning from their mistakes and rebuilding wisely, those who experience relationship fraud can heal, grow, and emerge stronger than before. This chapter explores the recovery process, from acknowledging the damage to rebuilding self-trust and opening up to healthier relationships.

5.1 Recovery and Emotional Rehabilitation

The first step in healing is acknowledging what happened without self-blame. Many victims of emotional fraud experience guilt, shame, and self-doubt, wondering if they were foolish for falling into the trap.

<u>Step 1: Acknowledging the Scam Without Blaming Yourself</u>

You were not stupid—manipulators are skilled at deception.

You were not weak—you simply trusted someone who didn't deserve it.

You were not unworthy—their inability to sustain love is not a reflection of your value.

Fraud victims often feel embarrassed about being deceived, but healing begins when you recognize that being manipulated does not make you the problem. It simply means you placed trust in someone who wasn't worthy of it.

<u>Step 2: Cutting Off All Contact to Break the Cycle</u>

The first rule of financial fraud recovery is to cut ties with the scammer—no more money, no more investments, no more conversations.

The same applies to emotional fraud: No Contact is key.

Why? Because fraudsters always try to return when they need another "investment."

Common manipulative tactics they use post-breakup:

"I miss you."

"I realized I made a mistake."

"Can we just talk?"

"I still love you, but I need time."

This is the Hoovering Tactic—designed to suck you back in and restart the cycle. Do not engage.

<u>Step 3: Processing the Grief and Emotional Loss</u>

Even if the relationship was toxic, losing it still hurts. It's the loss of a dream, the loss of expectations, and sometimes, the loss of self-identity.

How to Process Emotional Loss Effectively:

Accept that healing isn't linear – Some days you'll feel fine, other days you'll feel like you're back at square one. That's normal.

Write it out – Journaling your emotions helps make sense of them and prevents you from bottling them up.

Seek therapy if needed – Just as financial fraud victims seek legal help, emotional fraud victims can benefit from professional guidance.

Allow yourself to grieve – The relationship may have been an illusion, but your emotions were real. Processing them is essential to healing.

5.2 Love with a New Perspective – Smarter Investments

Once you have healed from the emotional collapse, the next step is to change your relationship approach so you don't fall into another Ponzi scheme.

<u>Step 4: Building Self-Worth Without External Validation</u>

Many victims of emotional fraud were targeted because they sought validation from their partner. The manipulator exploited this need, providing just enough love to keep them hooked while slowly withdrawing.

The best way to prevent this from happening again? Become your own best investor.

Ways to Build Self-Worth Independently:

? Practice self-care that isn't relationship-dependent (hobbies, fitness, travel, creative pursuits).

? Develop emotional independence—learn to enjoy your own company.

? Set standards and enforce them—define your relationship boundaries.

? Avoid making love your only source of happiness—fulfillment should come from multiple areas of life.

<u>Step 5: Identifying and Avoiding Future Relationship Scams</u>

Now that you've rebuilt your confidence, it's time to change your relationship investment strategy.

? Slow down the investment process – Take your time before committing fully.

? Observe consistency – Do their actions match their words over time?

? Watch for cycles of intense affection followed by withdrawal – This is a classic scam pattern.

? Trust your gut – If something feels off, don't ignore it.

Key Relationship Rule: Love should feel like a stable, sustainable business—not a high-risk, get-rich-quick scheme.

5.3 The Long-Term View: Love as a Healthy Investment

The final step in the recovery process is shifting from scarcity mindset to abundance mindset.

In financial fraud cases, victims often feel they've lost everything, but successful recovery comes from realizing that new opportunities always exist.

The same applies to love.

<u>Step 6: Moving from Scarcity to Abundance in Relationships</u>

Scarcity mindset: "I'll never find someone else. Love is hard to come by."

Abundance mindset: "Healthy love exists, and I don't need to settle for less."

People who fall into love scams often believe that love is rare—that's why they tolerate toxicity. But love isn't scarce. What's scarce is authenticity, consistency, and emotional stability.

Creating a Future of Healthy Love

Set a Standard for Future Relationships – Define what healthy love looks like for you.

Develop Emotional Wealth – Just as financial stability attracts better investments, emotional stability attracts healthier partners.

Invest in the Right People – Give your time and energy only to those who show consistent reciprocity.

Conclusion: From Victim to Victor

The final transformation from victim to victor comes when you realize:

? You didn't lose—it was a lesson, not a failure.

? Your self-worth isn't determined by someone else's ability to love you.

? You have the power to choose who you invest in—and you will never invest in another Ponzi scheme.

Much like financial fraud victims who rebuild their fortunes smarter and stronger, emotional fraud victims can rebuild their love lives with wisdom and strength.

Love, when built on authenticity, mutual effort, and emotional stability, is the most rewarding investment of all.

Familial Love & Relationships: The Fine Line Between Support & Obligation

CHAPTER SIXTEEN

UNDERSTANDING FAMILIAL LOVE & ITS EVOLUTION

1.1 The Concept of Familial Love Across Cultures

Familial love is often considered one of the purest and most selfless forms of love. It forms the foundation of human relationships and is deeply ingrained in cultural, social, and religious traditions worldwide. However, the way this love is expressed and expected varies significantly across cultures.

In collectivist societies, such as those in Asia, Africa, and Latin America, familial love is closely tied to duty, respect, and interdependence. Family members are expected to support each other financially, emotionally, and socially, often placing family needs above individual aspirations. Elders are highly respected, and multi-generational households are common, reinforcing the idea that family is not just about emotional bonds but also a lifelong obligation.

Conversely, in individualistic cultures like those in Western Europe and North America, familial love is often viewed through the lens of personal freedom and mutual respect rather than obligation. While family bonds are still valued, there is an emphasis on independence, with children encouraged to leave home and build their own lives without the expectation of lifelong financial or caretaking responsibilities for their parents.

The evolving definition of family also reflects cultural shifts. Traditional nuclear families—consisting of two parents and their children—are no longer the sole norm. Blended families, single-parent households, same-sex parenting, and chosen families (close friends who take on familial roles) are increasingly recognized as legitimate expressions of familial love.

1.2 The Psychology Behind Family Bonds

The human need for connection is deeply rooted in psychology. Attachment theory, developed by John Bowlby, suggests that early bonds with caregivers shape our ability to form relationships throughout life. Secure attachments in childhood lead to healthier emotional regulation and interpersonal relationships, while insecure attachments can result in dependency issues or emotional detachment.

Psychologists have long studied how familial love impacts emotional well-being. Studies show that strong family support systems lead to lower stress levels, better mental health, and increased resilience in times of crisis. However, the opposite is also true: dysfunctional family dynamics can lead to anxiety, depression, and long-term emotional scars.

The balance between love and autonomy is one of the most complex aspects of family relationships. Parents, for example, must strike a delicate balance between providing care and allowing independence. Overprotectiveness can hinder a child's ability to develop confidence and problem-solving skills, while neglect can lead to feelings of insecurity and abandonment.

Sibling relationships are also shaped by psychology. Birth order, parental favoritism, and early childhood dynamics can create lifelong patterns of rivalry, camaraderie, or distance. While some siblings become each other's greatest support systems, others struggle with unresolved childhood conflicts that persist into adulthood.

1.3 Expectations vs. Reality in Family Roles

The concept of family roles has traditionally been defined by societal norms. Parents are expected to nurture and guide, children are expected to obey and respect, and siblings are expected to support each other. However, these expectations are often idealistic and do not always align with reality.

<u>Parental Expectations</u>

Parents often have a vision of their children's future that may not match the child's aspirations. This can lead to conflicts, especially in cultures where parental authority is deeply respected. For instance, career choices, marriage, and lifestyle decisions can become points of contention. The expectation that children must "repay" their parents' sacrifices by fulfilling their desires can create emotional burdens.

Additionally, the role reversal in old age—where children become caregivers to their parents—brings new complexities. While some individuals willingly take on this responsibility, others may feel burdened, particularly if financial or emotional resources are limited.

<u>Sibling Dynamics</u>

The idea that siblings should always support each other is another expectation that does not always hold. While many siblings share close bonds, others may experience rivalry, resentment, or emotional distance due to favoritism, inheritance disputes, or personality differences. In some families, the eldest child is expected to take on a quasi-parental role, bearing the responsibility of looking after younger siblings even into adulthood.

<u>Extended Family & Social Obligations</u>

In many cultures, family obligations extend beyond the immediate household. Uncles, aunts, cousins, and even distant relatives may expect financial or emotional support. The idea of "family duty" can sometimes place immense pressure on individuals, making it difficult to prioritize personal goals.

The gap between expectation and reality often leads to guilt, frustration, and even estrangement. While love should be the foundation of family relationships, it is often entangled with duty, making it difficult to distinguish genuine affection from societal pressure.

Conclusion

Familial love is a powerful force that shapes our identities, values, and life choices. However, it is not always free from expectations, obligations, and societal pressures. Understanding the evolution of familial love—from cultural variations to psychological impacts—helps us navigate our relationships with greater awareness and emotional intelligence.

As we move forward in the discussion, we will explore where the fine line between love and obligation begins to blur and how individuals can establish healthy boundaries while maintaining strong family ties.

CHAPTER SEVENTEEN

THE BURDEN OF OBLIGATION – WHERE DOES SUPPORT END?

2.1 The Silent Pressure of Family Expectations

Family expectations often manifest in ways that are not explicitly stated but deeply understood. From a young age, individuals are taught that familial bonds come with unspoken duties—taking care of parents in old age, financially supporting siblings, or upholding family traditions. This silent pressure can weigh heavily on individuals, influencing major life decisions such as career choices, marriage, and financial planning.

In some cultures, the eldest child is expected to be the family's pillar of support, assuming responsibilities that may come at the cost of personal ambitions. Even in more egalitarian societies, there is often a lingering expectation that family members must "show up" regardless of personal limitations or desires. When these expectations are not met, they can lead to feelings of guilt, disappointment, and fractured relationships.

Beyond financial responsibilities, emotional labor is another aspect of familial expectations. Individuals may be expected to be the peacemaker, the decision-maker, or the caregiver in times of crisis, often at the expense of their own mental well-being. This invisible burden can create an imbalance where one person consistently bears more weight than others in the family.

2.2 Guilt, Sacrifice & Emotional Manipulation

One of the strongest emotional tools in family obligation is guilt. Statements like "After all we've done for you" or "You owe us this much" can create a sense of indebtedness, making it difficult for individuals to set boundaries. Sacrifice becomes an unspoken currency in family relationships—one person giving up their dreams for the collective benefit of others.

Emotional manipulation, whether intentional or subconscious, can also be a factor. Parents may place undue pressure on children to meet expectations, siblings may leverage emotional closeness to demand favors, and extended family members may subtly enforce cultural norms that make saying no feel impossible. These dynamics often result in individuals prioritizing family demands over personal happiness, leading to resentment and burnout.

For instance, a daughter may feel compelled to put her career on hold to care for aging parents, even if she has aspirations of her own. Similarly, a son might be pressured into financially supporting his siblings at the cost of his own financial security. While familial love often involves sacrifice, the problem arises when the sacrifice is expected rather than given willingly.

Cultural and societal norms further perpetuate this cycle. In some communities, children—especially women—are conditioned to prioritize family duties over personal fulfillment. This can lead to long-term emotional struggles, where individuals grapple with feelings of obligation versus their own desires.

2.3 When Love Becomes a Duty

At what point does love transform from a genuine emotion to an obligatory duty? There is a fine line between supporting family out of love and feeling forced to do so out of obligation. While it is natural to care for loved ones, the expectation that one must always be available can erode personal freedom.

Elder care is one area where this transition becomes particularly evident. While some individuals willingly take on the responsibility of looking after aging parents, others may feel obligated despite lacking the resources or emotional capacity to do so. Similarly, financial support for struggling family members, while often given with good intentions, can turn into a perpetual expectation rather than a voluntary act of kindness.

This transition from love to duty can also impact mental and emotional well-being. People who constantly meet family obligations out of pressure rather than choice may develop feelings of resentment, depression, or even burnout. The expectation to always prioritize family can make it difficult for individuals to establish personal goals, pursue careers, or build relationships outside of their family unit.

2.4 Financial Burdens and Unfair Expectations

Money is often a major factor in familial obligations. Whether it's sending money back home, supporting a sibling's education, or funding a family business, financial burdens can create long-term stress and strain relationships. In some cases, individuals are expected to bear these costs simply because they are perceived to be more financially stable.

Many people feel trapped in a cycle where they cannot say no to financial demands from their family without experiencing immense guilt. This expectation is especially common in collectivist cultures, where financial success is often seen as a shared achievement rather than an individual accomplishment.

Financial dependency can also create imbalances within a family. One sibling may end up shouldering the responsibility of supporting parents while others contribute little. This uneven dynamic can lead to resentment and conflict, making it crucial for families to have open discussions about financial fairness and realistic expectations.

2.5 The Emotional Toll of Perpetual Obligation

The weight of constant familial obligations can lead to severe emotional and psychological consequences. Many individuals struggle with anxiety, stress, and emotional exhaustion due to the feeling that they must always be available to meet their family's needs.

People who experience extreme obligation may also find it difficult to maintain personal relationships outside of their family. The expectation to prioritize family above all else can hinder the ability to build romantic partnerships, friendships, and independent social circles.

Setting boundaries becomes a critical skill in managing these pressures. Learning to say no without guilt, communicating personal limits effectively, and finding ways to support family without sacrificing oneself are essential steps in maintaining a healthy balance.

2.6 How to Set Boundaries Without Guilt

Navigating family obligations while maintaining independence requires clear and healthy boundaries. Here are some strategies to help individuals manage their family responsibilities without feeling overwhelmed:

Recognize Unhealthy Patterns – Identifying when obligation turns into manipulation or undue pressure is the first step toward change.

Communicate Openly – Honest discussions with family members about limitations and personal priorities can prevent misunderstandings.

Prioritize Self-Care – Recognizing that taking care of oneself is not selfish but necessary for long-term well-being.

Set Financial Boundaries – Helping family should not come at the cost of one's own financial stability.

Seek Support – Talking to a therapist, mentor, or trusted friend can provide guidance in managing family dynamics.

2.7 Moving Forward: Finding a Balance

Familial love and obligation are deeply interconnected, but they should not come at the cost of personal freedom and happiness. Striking a balance between supporting family and maintaining personal autonomy is possible with open communication, self-awareness, and healthy boundary-setting.

At the heart of family relationships should be mutual respect and understanding. True love does not demand sacrifice at the expense of one's well-being but allows for both support and personal growth. By redefining familial responsibilities in a way that is fair and sustainable, individuals can nurture meaningful relationships without being burdened by unrealistic expectations.

Understanding the thin line between support and obligation helps individuals reclaim agency over their lives while still honoring the love they have for their family. Ultimately, finding a middle ground where both love and individual needs coexist is the key to maintaining healthy and fulfilling family relationships.

CHAPTER EIGHTEEN

Setting Boundaries Without Losing Family Bonds

3.1 The Importance of Healthy Boundaries

Family relationships are among the most significant in our lives, shaping our emotional and psychological well-being. However, these relationships can become strained when clear boundaries are not set. Boundaries are essential for maintaining a sense of personal autonomy while still nurturing close family bonds. Without them, relationships can become enmeshed, leading to stress, resentment, and an imbalance in emotional and physical responsibilities.

A boundary is essentially a personal limit that helps define how we engage with others. When applied in family dynamics, they ensure that love and support remain voluntary rather than obligatory. Boundaries allow individuals to balance their roles within the family without feeling overwhelmed by obligations they did not choose.

Signs That Boundaries Are Needed

Feeling drained or exhausted after family interactions.

Constantly putting family needs above personal well-being.

Experiencing guilt for prioritizing personal desires.

Dealing with excessive criticism, control, or emotional manipulation.

Being financially or emotionally overburdened by family expectations.

Understanding the importance of boundaries and recognizing the signs that they are needed is the first step in maintaining healthy family relationships while protecting one's mental and emotional health.

3.2 How to Establish and Communicate Boundaries

Setting boundaries is not about shutting out family members; rather, it is about creating a structure that fosters respect and mutual understanding. The key to setting boundaries successfully is clear and compassionate communication.

<u>1. Define Your Boundaries Clearly</u>

Before discussing boundaries with family members, take time to reflect on your needs. Identify the areas in your life where family involvement has become overwhelming or intrusive. Boundaries can be set in different areas, including:

Time: How much time you can realistically dedicate to family gatherings or obligations.

Emotions: Avoiding conversations or interactions that cause unnecessary stress or anxiety.

Finances: Setting limits on financial support provided to family members.

Personal Space: Ensuring you have the physical or emotional distance needed to maintain balance.

<u>2. Communicate Boundaries with Respect</u>

Once you've established your boundaries, discuss them openly with family members. The key to a successful conversation is using clear and direct language while remaining respectful.

Use "I" statements to express your feelings and needs (e.g., "I need time to focus on my personal projects, so I won't be available every weekend.")

Avoid blaming or making accusations, which may lead to defensiveness.

Acknowledge their perspective but remain firm in your stance.

<u>3. Anticipate Resistance and Stay Firm</u>

When setting boundaries, it is common to experience pushback, especially if family members are accustomed to a certain level of access and influence over your life. Some may react with guilt-tripping, passive aggression, or outright rejection of your requests. It is important to:

Reaffirm your commitment to the relationship while maintaining your boundary.

Avoid engaging in emotional manipulation tactics.

Remind yourself why you set the boundary in the first place.

Be prepared to enforce consequences if boundaries continue to be ignored.

3.3 Maintaining Boundaries Without Guilt

One of the biggest challenges in setting boundaries with family is overcoming the guilt associated with prioritizing oneself. Many people fear that enforcing boundaries will lead to emotional distance or strained relationships. However, boundaries strengthen relationships by fostering mutual respect and understanding.

<u>Overcoming Guilt</u>

Acknowledge that you are not responsible for other people's feelings. Family members may feel disappointed or frustrated, but their emotions are theirs to manage.

Understand that prioritizing yourself is not selfish. Just as you support your family, you also deserve support and self-care.

Reframe your perspective. Instead of seeing boundaries as exclusionary, view them as a means to maintain healthier, more sustainable relationships.

Practice self-compassion. Remind yourself that you deserve personal space, time, and emotional well-being.

<u>How to Handle Guilt Traps</u>

Guilt-tripping is a common reaction when boundaries are first set. Family members may say things like:

"After everything I've done for you, this is how you treat me?"

"We're family; you should always put family first."

"You don't care about us anymore."

Instead of reacting emotionally, respond calmly and reinforce your boundary:

"I love and appreciate everything you've done for me, but I need to take care of my well-being too."

"I am here for you, but I also have to balance other responsibilities."

"I value our relationship, and having these boundaries helps me be more present and supportive."

3.4 Handling Toxic Family Dynamics

Not all family relationships are healthy. Some are toxic, filled with manipulation, control, or emotional abuse. In such cases, stronger boundaries—or even distancing yourself—may be necessary.

<u>Recognizing Toxic Family Patterns</u>

Constant criticism or belittling.

Emotional manipulation through guilt, anger, or silent treatment.

Excessive control over life decisions.

Repetitive cycles of conflict with no resolution.

Disrespect for personal space, choices, or individuality.

<u>How to Navigate Toxic Family Relationships</u>

Limit interactions. Reduce exposure to toxic family members if direct confrontation is ineffective.

Be selective with what you share. Protect your privacy to avoid unnecessary interference in your life.

Seek external support. Therapy, support groups, or trusted friends can provide guidance on handling difficult family dynamics.

Consider distancing or cutting ties if necessary. In extreme cases where emotional well-being is severely impacted, detaching from toxic family members may be the healthiest choice.

3.5 Strengthening Family Bonds While Maintaining Boundaries

Boundaries should not create emotional distance; rather, they should foster deeper, healthier connections. Here's how to ensure that setting boundaries doesn't damage family relationships:

<u>1. Find Middle Ground</u>

If your family struggles to accept your boundaries, try compromising where possible while still prioritizing your needs. For example, if they expect daily calls, propose weekly check-ins instead.

<u>2. Reinforce Positive Interactions</u>

Instead of focusing only on boundaries, make an effort to engage in positive interactions. Spend quality time together in ways that feel comfortable and fulfilling for both parties.

<u>3. Educate Your Family About Boundaries</u>

Many families do not understand the concept of boundaries. Helping them see that setting boundaries benefits everyone in the long run can lead to better acceptance.

<u>4. Lead by Example</u>

Model the behavior you want to see in your family. Respect their boundaries as well, showing that setting limits is a two-way street that enhances relationships.

Conclusion

Setting boundaries with family is a crucial step toward achieving a balanced and fulfilling life. While it may initially feel uncomfortable or even selfish, boundaries are a sign of self-respect and maturity. By defining personal limits, communicating them with clarity, and reinforcing them with consistency, individuals can maintain strong family bonds without losing their sense of self.

True familial love is not about sacrifice at the expense of personal well-being—it is about mutual respect, understanding, and the ability to support each other without feeling obligated. When done right, boundaries do not push family members apart; they bring them closer by creating a healthier and more sustainable way to connect and care for one another.

CHAPTER NINETEEN

Navigating Crises & Difficult Family Situations

4.1 Family Conflicts: The Role of Communication

Family conflicts are inevitable, as each individual has unique perspectives, emotions, and expectations. Effective communication is the cornerstone of resolving disputes and maintaining family harmony. However, many families struggle with healthy communication, often resorting to avoidance, passive-aggression, or outright hostility.

<u>Common Sources of Family Conflicts</u>

Financial issues: Disagreements over inheritance, shared expenses, or financial support.

Differing values and beliefs: Generational or cultural gaps leading to misunderstandings.

Parental favoritism: Perceived or real unequal treatment among siblings.

Life choices: Disapproval of career, relationship, or lifestyle decisions.

Unresolved past conflicts: Lingering resentment over past events or grievances.

<u>Strategies for Effective Communication</u>

Active listening: Show empathy by listening without interrupting or forming counterarguments.

Use "I" statements: Express feelings without placing blame (e.g., "I feel hurt when...").

Set discussion boundaries: Avoid yelling, personal attacks, or bringing up past mistakes.

Timing is key: Address conflicts when emotions have settled to ensure a productive conversation.

Seek mediation: A neutral third party (therapist, elder, or mediator) can help navigate disputes.

4.2 Dealing with Estrangement & Unresolved Issues

Not all family conflicts can be resolved, and in some cases, estrangement may become necessary for emotional well-being. However, navigating estrangement is a deeply personal and emotionally complex experience.

<u>Understanding Estrangement</u>

Estrangement does not always mean a complete severance of ties. It may involve setting firm boundaries, reducing contact, or opting for limited communication to protect one's mental and emotional health.

Steps to Navigate Estrangement

Assess the necessity: Is estrangement truly the best option, or can the relationship be repaired with boundaries?

Communicate your decision: If possible, calmly explain why you are choosing to distance yourself.

Seek emotional support: Therapy or support groups can help manage guilt and grief.

Be prepared for reactions: Family members may not accept your decision immediately.

Revisit the decision over time: Some estrangements may be temporary; reassess if circumstances change.

4.3 Balancing Personal Goals & Family Responsibilities

Balancing personal ambitions while fulfilling family responsibilities is one of the most difficult aspects of family life. Many individuals struggle with guilt when prioritizing personal goals over family expectations.

<u>Common Family Responsibilities</u>

Financial support: Providing for parents, siblings, or extended family.

Caregiving: Taking care of elderly, sick, or dependent family members.

Emotional availability: Constantly being the go-to person for family problems.

Upholding traditions: Meeting cultural or religious expectations despite personal beliefs.

<u>Strategies for Finding Balance</u>

Communicate openly: Explain your goals and limitations clearly to family members.

Delegate responsibilities: If possible, distribute duties among multiple family members.

Prioritize self-care: Recognize that taking care of yourself enables you to support others effectively.

Set financial boundaries: Offer support without compromising your financial stability.

Reassess commitments regularly: Evaluate what is sustainable for your mental and physical well-being.

4.4 Coping with Family Tragedies & Loss

Grief and loss are among the most challenging experiences within a family. Whether it's the passing of a loved one, a major health crisis, or an unforeseen disaster, navigating these moments requires strength, support, and understanding.

<u>Stages of Grief in Families</u>

Grief impacts each family member differently. Some may express their emotions openly, while others may withdraw. Understanding *the five stages of grief (denial, anger, bargaining, depression, acceptance)* can help in navigating collective grief within a family.

<u>How to Support Each Other During Tragedies</u>

Allow space for different grieving styles: Respect that not everyone processes loss in the same way.

Communicate and check in regularly: Even if words feel insufficient, showing support matters.

Avoid placing blame: In times of crisis, tension can lead to misplaced blame; focus on healing instead.

Seek professional help: Family counseling or grief support groups can aid in the healing process.

Honor memories together: Finding ways to commemorate lost loved ones can help with closure.

4.5 Managing Crisis Situations Without Breaking Family Bonds

Families often face crises, such as financial hardships, major health issues, or sudden relocations. How these situations are handled determines whether they strengthen or strain family bonds.

<u>How to Handle a Family Crisis Constructively</u>

Stay calm and assess the situation: Avoid impulsive reactions.

Create a support plan: Divide responsibilities to prevent overwhelming a single family member.

Keep communication open: Ensure that everyone understands the crisis and potential solutions.

Be flexible: Crises require adaptability; be open to adjusting plans and roles.

Seek external resources: Community support, financial aid, or therapy can help in managing crisis situations.

Conclusion

Navigating crises and difficult family situations requires emotional intelligence, patience, and a willingness to adapt. By fostering open communication, setting realistic expectations, and prioritizing well-being, individuals can navigate family hardships without losing themselves in the process. While some situations may call for distance or boundary-setting, others provide opportunities for growth and strengthened familial bonds. The key lies in finding a balance that respects both individual needs and family unity.

CHAPTER TWENTY

REDEFINING FAMILIAL LOVE IN THE MODERN WORLD

5.1 The Changing Definition of Family

As societies evolve, so does the definition of family. Traditional family structures, once rigidly defined by cultural and societal norms, are now being reshaped by changing values, technological advancements, and shifting social dynamics. The modern world has seen the rise of non-traditional family models, including single-parent households, same-sex parenting, blended families, and chosen families—groups of individuals who create strong, familial-like bonds despite not being related by blood.

<u>Factors Influencing the Evolution of Family</u>

Technology & Communication: Digital platforms enable family members to stay connected despite geographical distances.

Legal & Social Recognition: Many countries now recognize same-sex marriage and provide legal protections for diverse family structures.

Economic Factors: Rising costs of living influence multigenerational households and alternative living arrangements.

Cultural Shifts: Societies are becoming more accepting of non-traditional family models, focusing on emotional bonds rather than rigid structures.

5.2 The Art of Loving Without Losing Yourself

One of the most challenging aspects of familial love is balancing emotional investment with self-preservation. Many individuals struggle with prioritizing their personal aspirations while meeting family expectations. The key lies in understanding that familial love should not come at the expense of one's well-being.

<u>How to Maintain Individuality in Family Relationships</u>

Establish Personal Goals: Define your own life ambitions separate from familial expectations.

Set Emotional Boundaries: Recognize when familial obligations become burdens rather than mutual support.

Prioritize Mental Well-being: Engage in self-care without guilt, knowing that you cannot pour from an empty cup.

Communicate Openly: Express personal needs while respecting family values and traditions.

5.3 The Role of Emotional Intelligence in Modern Families

Emotional intelligence (EI) plays a crucial role in strengthening modern family bonds. EI allows individuals to navigate difficult conversations, manage conflicts effectively, and cultivate deep, lasting relationships. Families that encourage emotional intelligence tend to foster healthier communication and stronger support systems.

<u>Key Components of Emotional Intelligence in Families</u>

Self-Awareness: Recognizing and understanding your own emotions before reacting impulsively.

Empathy: Understanding and validating the emotions of family members.

Conflict Resolution Skills: Approaching disagreements with a problem-solving mindset rather than confrontation.

Adaptability: Adjusting to changing family dynamics with an open mind.

5.4 Building a Family Culture of Support, Not Obligation

A significant shift in modern familial relationships is the move away from obligation-based interactions towards support-based relationships. In many traditional settings, familial love is often associated with duty—children are expected to care for parents, siblings must support one another financially, and sacrifices are normalized. However, the modern world calls for a balance where family relationships thrive on mutual respect and voluntary support rather than forced obligations.

<u>How to Foster a Healthy Family Culture</u>

Encourage Independence: Support family members in pursuing their own aspirations without guilt.

Normalize Open Discussions: Create a safe space for family members to express concerns and needs without judgment.

Recognize and Respect Boundaries: Understand that unconditional love does not mean unlimited access to each other's time and resources.

Celebrate Individual Achievements: Acknowledge each person's growth without comparison or unrealistic expectations.

5.5 The Future of Familial Love: Adaptation and Resilience

The future of familial love lies in its ability to adapt. As people live longer, relocate more frequently, and redefine personal fulfillment, family structures must become more resilient to these changes. Relationships that thrive are those that evolve with time, adjusting to the needs and aspirations of each individual rather than relying on outdated traditions.

<u>Predictions for Future Family Dynamics</u>

Greater Flexibility in Roles: Less emphasis on traditional gender roles and responsibilities.

Technology-Driven Connection: Virtual family gatherings and digital communication replacing physical proximity.

Legal and Social Changes: More inclusive definitions of family to accommodate diverse relationships.

Holistic Family Well-being: Focus on collective emotional, mental, and financial well-being rather than individual sacrifices.

Conclusion

Familial love in the modern world is not about rigid traditions but about mutual understanding, emotional intelligence, and voluntary support. Redefining family relationships allows individuals to maintain a sense of self while fostering meaningful connections. As society continues to evolve, so must our approach to family—adapting, growing, and ensuring that love remains a source of strength rather than obligation.

Friendships & Social Circles: Not All Networks Are Net Gains

CHAPTER TWENTY-ONE

THE FOUNDATIONS OF FRIENDSHIP & SOCIAL CIRCLES

1.1 Understanding the Essence of Friendship

Friendship is one of the most profound relationships humans can cultivate. It is built on mutual trust, respect, and shared experiences. Unlike familial relationships, which are formed by birth, friendships are chosen bonds, making them unique in their depth and significance.

Psychologists define friendship as a close, voluntary relationship that provides emotional support, companionship, and a sense of belonging. While some friendships develop organically over time, others require intentional effort to nurture and sustain.

<u>The Psychology of Friendship</u>

Friendships are essential for mental and emotional well-being. Research suggests that strong friendships lead to lower stress levels, improved self-esteem, and better overall life satisfaction. Studies also show that friendships activate the brain's reward system, releasing oxytocin and dopamine—chemicals that enhance happiness and trust.

<u>Types of Friendships</u>

Friendships can take different forms depending on context, personality, and life circumstances:

Childhood Friendships: Often formed in school or neighborhoods, these relationships lay the foundation for social skills and trust-building.

Work Friendships: Built in professional environments, these friendships help individuals navigate workplace dynamics and foster collaboration.

Digital Friendships: With the rise of social media, online communities have enabled connections across geographic barriers, though these relationships can sometimes lack depth.

Situational Friendships: These develop based on shared circumstances, such as gym buddies, travel acquaintances, or conference networking.

Regardless of the type, friendships require reciprocity, empathy, and mutual effort to thrive.

1.2 The Role of Social Circles in Personal and Professional Growth

Social circles refer to the larger network of relationships that extend beyond close friendships. These networks play a crucial role in shaping one's personal and professional journey.

<u>The Importance of Social Support</u>

A strong social circle provides emotional and practical support. Whether it's celebrating achievements, offering encouragement during tough times, or providing advice, a well-rounded social network enhances resilience and motivation.

How Social Circles Shape Identity and Perspectives

People are greatly influenced by those they interact with regularly. Social psychologist David McClelland suggests that individuals are the average of the five people they spend the most time with.

Personal Growth: Exposure to diverse perspectives fosters intellectual and emotional development.

Professional Opportunities: Networking within the right circles can lead to career advancements and business opportunities.

Behavioral Influence: Social groups shape habits, from lifestyle choices to decision-making approaches.

Balancing Close Friendships and Larger Social Networks

While close friendships provide depth and emotional security, larger social networks offer breadth and opportunities. Finding a balance between deep relationships and broader connections ensures a fulfilling social life.

1.3 The Changing Nature of Friendships Over Time

Friendships evolve as individuals move through different life stages. What begins as childhood companionship may transition into distant acquaintanceship due to life changes.

<u>Life Stages and Friendship Dynamics</u>

Adolescence: Friendships in teenage years are intense and emotional, often influenced by shared activities and peer validation.

Early Adulthood: As careers and responsibilities take precedence, friendships become more selective and intentional.

Mid-Life Friendships: Family and professional commitments often limit social interactions, making quality over quantity a priority.

Later Years: Friendships become essential for companionship and emotional well-being, especially after retirement.

Major Shifts in Social Circles

Friendships are often affected by life transitions such as:

College and Career Changes: Moving to a new city or job can reshape social circles.

Marriage and Parenthood: Family responsibilities can shift the focus from friendships to household priorities.

Health and Aging: Physical limitations may impact social interactions, making virtual connections more common.

The Impact of Globalization and Digitalization on Social Connections

With globalization, friendships are no longer confined to local communities. The digital age allows individuals to maintain long-distance friendships and build online communities. However, the downside is that virtual interactions can sometimes lack emotional depth compared to in-person relationships.

Conclusion

Friendships and social circles are fundamental to personal and professional well-being. They shape identity, provide emotional support, and influence decision-making. However, as life evolves, so do these relationships. Understanding the foundations of friendships helps in making intentional choices about who to surround oneself with, ensuring meaningful and enriching social connections.

CHAPTER TWENTY-TWO

THE HIDDEN COSTS OF FRIENDSHIPS & NETWORKING

2.1 When Friendships Become Emotional Liabilities

Friendships are often seen as sources of joy and emotional support, but not all friendships are equally rewarding. Some friendships, rather than being uplifting, can become emotional liabilities that drain energy, create stress, and hinder personal growth. Understanding when and how friendships cross this line is crucial to maintaining emotional well-being.

<u>Emotional Drain from One-Sided Friendships</u>

A healthy friendship is based on mutual effort and care. However, some friendships become imbalanced when one person consistently gives while the other takes without reciprocation.

Signs of a one-sided friendship:

Always initiating conversations or plans without the other making an effort.

Feeling emotionally exhausted after interactions.

Lack of interest or support from the other person when you need them.

Being used as a constant emotional dumping ground without receiving the same consideration.

Consequences:

Burnout from emotional labor.

Decreased self-worth due to feeling undervalued.

Anxiety or resentment towards the friendship.

Dealing with Toxic or Manipulative Friends

Some friendships go beyond emotional imbalance and turn toxic. Toxic friends can be manipulative, controlling, or exploitative, leaving you feeling worse rather than better after interactions.

Red flags in toxic friendships:

They guilt-trip or manipulate you into doing things for them.

They dismiss your feelings while making their problems the focus.

They thrive on gossip or negativity.

They undermine your confidence and decisions.

<u>Emotional Dependency vs. Genuine Care</u>

Friendships should be about mutual emotional support, not dependency. Emotional dependency occurs when one person relies too heavily on the other for validation, decision-making, or even happiness.

Differentiating emotional dependency from healthy support:

Healthy friendships encourage independence and growth.

Emotional dependency leads to clinginess and feelings of suffocation.

True friends respect personal boundaries and do not make excessive demands.

2.2 Social Circles & Peer Pressure: The Unseen Manipulation

Social circles significantly influence behavior, choices, and life directions. While they can provide valuable support, they can also exert invisible pressures that manipulate individuals into making decisions they otherwise wouldn't.

<u>How Friend Groups Shape Habits and Decisions</u>

Our social circles influence our habits, from health choices to financial behaviors. Friends can unconsciously push us toward behaviors we wouldn't engage in alone, both positive and negative.

Examples of social influence:

Adopting spending habits based on peers.

Engaging in unhealthy behaviors like excessive drinking or reckless spending.

Making career or life decisions based on peer trends rather than personal aspirations.

<u>Recognizing Negative Peer Pressure</u>

Peer pressure isn't always overt. It can be subtle, making it harder to identify until it has already shaped one's actions.

Subtle peer pressure tactics:

The fear of missing out (FOMO) causing unnecessary commitments.

Unspoken competition in achievements, lifestyle, or wealth.

The need to conform to group norms even if they go against personal values.

<u>Breaking Free from Unhealthy Social Dynamics</u>

Understanding how to break free from negative peer influence is essential to making independent and meaningful life choices.

Steps to regain control:

Practicing assertiveness to resist undue influence.

Finding like-minded individuals who align with your values.

Setting firm personal boundaries without guilt.

2.3 The Burden of Social Expectations

Society imposes expectations on how people should behave in friendships and networking circles. While maintaining social harmony is important, conforming too much can lead to personal dissatisfaction and frustration.

<u>Social Obligations and the Stress of Keeping Up Appearances</u>

Many people engage in social activities out of obligation rather than genuine interest. This creates stress, drains energy, and reduces time for self-care.

Signs of unhealthy social obligations:

Feeling forced to attend events or gatherings.

Engaging in small talk or superficial relationships out of duty.

Feeling guilty for not keeping up with every social interaction.

Strategies to manage social obligations:

Prioritizing genuine connections over superficial interactions.

Politely declining invitations that don't add value to your life.

Practicing selective socializing to reduce mental fatigue.

<u>The Fine Line Between Social Politeness and Being Exploited</u>

Being polite and accommodating is often valued in social settings, but it can be exploited by those who take advantage of kindness.

Recognizing social exploitation:

People who only reach out when they need something.

Always being the one who makes sacrifices in a group.

Being pressured to comply with unreasonable demands to maintain peace.

How to assert yourself without conflict:

Learning to say no without feeling guilty.

Communicating boundaries in a clear but respectful manner.

Distancing yourself from people who habitually exploit generosity.

<u>Saying 'No' Without Guilt: Setting Healthy Boundaries</u>
Boundaries protect mental and emotional well-being. Many people struggle with setting them due to fear of rejection or hurting others.

Steps to setting boundaries effectively:

Understanding personal limits and communicating them clearly.

Practicing self-respect without seeking external validation.

Replacing guilt with self-awareness and self-care.

Conclusion

Friendships and networking come with hidden costs that can drain emotional and mental energy. Recognizing when a relationship is becoming an emotional liability, understanding the subtle pressures of social circles, and setting healthy boundaries are crucial to maintaining a fulfilling social life. Prioritizing meaningful, balanced relationships over superficial or draining ones ensures long-term emotional well-being.

CHAPTER TWENTY-THREE

THE POWER & PITFALLS OF NETWORKING

3.1 Networking: More Than Just Making Connections

Networking is often viewed as a means to an end—climbing the professional ladder, securing business deals, or gaining influence. However, at its core, networking is about building meaningful relationships that provide mutual value.

<u>The Value of Networking in Professional Growth</u>

Networking is a critical skill in the modern world, opening doors to opportunities that may not be available through traditional channels. It plays a crucial role in career advancement, personal branding, and expanding knowledge.

<u>Professional Benefits of Networking:</u>

Access to Opportunities: Many job openings are never advertised, existing only in the "hidden job market."

Career Growth: Connections can offer mentorship, skill-building, and guidance.

Business Expansion: Entrepreneurs thrive on networking, forming partnerships, and identifying clients.

Knowledge Sharing: Staying informed about industry trends and best practices through peers.

<u>The Long-Term Value of Relationships:</u>

A strong network isn't just about short-term gains but long-term support.

Meaningful relationships often lead to unexpected career shifts and business ventures.

Mutual trust fosters opportunities beyond initial expectations.

<u>The Concept of Social Capital and Its Influence on Success</u>

Social capital is the collective value of social networks, encompassing trust, reciprocity, and shared resources. Unlike financial capital, social capital compounds over time.

Types of Social Capital:

Bonding Social Capital: Strong relationships within close-knit groups (family, close friends, colleagues).

Bridging Social Capital: Weak ties that connect different groups, often leading to new opportunities.

Linking Social Capital: Relationships with individuals in influential positions.

How to Cultivate Social Capital:

Build relationships based on mutual benefit, not just self-interest.

Engage in active listening and offer support before expecting favors.

Be consistent in maintaining connections, rather than reaching out only when in need.

3.2 When Networking Becomes Exploitative

While networking can be highly beneficial, it can also become manipulative or transactional. Many individuals fall into the trap of exploitative networking, where relationships are built solely for personal gain.

<u>Identifying Transactional Relationships</u>

A transactional relationship in networking lacks genuine connection and is based purely on what one person can get from the other.

Red Flags of Transactional Networking:

Someone only contacts you when they need something.

The relationship feels one-sided, with little reciprocity.

Conversations lack depth beyond professional or material interests.

Promises of support that never materialize.

<u>The Dangers of "Fake Friendships" for Professional Gain</u>

Many professionals fall into the trap of superficial friendships, where people pretend to care solely for personal benefit.

Negative Effects of Fake Friendships:

Loss of trust in professional relationships.

Emotional and mental exhaustion from maintaining superficial connections.

Damage to one's personal brand if exposed as insincere.

Missed opportunities for genuine mentorship and collaboration.

<u>How to Spot Red Flags in Networking Circles</u>

Not all networking circles are positive or beneficial. Some are exclusive, toxic, or demand more than they offer.

Signs of Unhealthy Networking Circles:

Overemphasis on status rather than meaningful engagement.

Cliquish behavior that excludes those not seen as immediately useful.

Pressure to conform to a group's standards, even at a personal cost.

Lack of genuine support for each other's goals and achievements.

<u>Escaping Toxic Networking Environments</u>

If networking becomes draining or exploitative, it may be time to step back or redefine your approach.

Ways to Exit Toxic Networks:

Gradually reduce participation and disengage from superficial interactions.

Focus on cultivating meaningful relationships outside of manipulative circles.

Set boundaries on how and when you engage with your network.

3.3 Selective Networking: Quality Over Quantity

Building a powerful network isn't about knowing the most people—it's about knowing the right people and fostering authentic connections.

<u>Curating a Social Network That Adds Value</u>

Selective networking ensures that the time and effort invested in connections yield genuine and mutually beneficial relationships.

Key Elements of a High-Quality Network:

Diversity in skills, industries, and perspectives.

Individuals who challenge and inspire growth.

Authentic relationships where both parties contribute equally.

How to Gracefully Exit Unproductive Networks

Not all connections are meant to last. If a network is not serving your growth, it's acceptable to disengage.

Steps to Let Go Without Burning Bridges:

Reduce interactions gradually rather than making abrupt exits.

Express gratitude for past interactions but redirect focus elsewhere.

Politely decline invitations to events or meetings that no longer align with your goals.

The Importance of Authenticity in Building Strong Connections

Being genuine in networking fosters deeper, more sustainable relationships. Authenticity strengthens trust and creates a reputation for integrity.

<u>Principles of Authentic Networking:</u>

Be honest about intentions and expectations in professional relationships.

Offer value to others before seeking personal benefits.

Engage in meaningful conversations rather than just exchanging business cards.

Follow up and maintain relationships with sincerity.

Conclusion: Balancing the Power and Pitfalls of Networking

Networking is a double-edged sword—it can be an incredible tool for professional and personal growth, but if misused, it can lead to exploitation and superficiality. The key to leveraging networking effectively lies in prioritizing authenticity, being selective with connections, and ensuring that relationships are built on mutual respect and genuine value. By focusing on quality over quantity, individuals can build meaningful networks that stand the test of time and truly contribute to their success.

CHAPTER TWENTY-FOUR

Identifying & Protecting Yourself from Toxic Social Dynamics

4.1 Recognizing Toxic Friendships & Social Groups

Not all friendships and social circles contribute positively to personal and professional growth. Some relationships become toxic, leading to emotional exhaustion, self-doubt, and unnecessary stress. Identifying these dynamics early can help in making healthier social choices.

<u>Traits of Toxic Friends</u>

A toxic friend can drain energy, manipulate emotions, and create an unhealthy dependence on their approval. Here are some common traits of toxic friendships:

Narcissistic Behavior: The relationship revolves around their needs and emotions, with little regard for yours.

Chronic Negativity: They constantly complain, criticize, or spread negativity, bringing down your mood.

Unreliability: They often break promises, cancel plans last minute, or fail to support you when needed.

Passive-Aggressiveness: They use indirect hostility, sarcasm, or silent treatment to manipulate situations.

Excessive Jealousy & Competitiveness: They feel envious of your success and may try to undermine your confidence.

<u>Red Flags in Social Circles</u>

While individuals can be toxic, entire social circles can also contribute to unhealthy behavior. Here's how to recognize toxic group dynamics:

Gossip Culture: A group that thrives on spreading rumors often fosters distrust and manipulation.

Exclusionary Behavior: Groups that frequently ostracize or belittle others create an unhealthy social environment.

Constant Drama: If conflicts and emotional turmoil are the norm, the group may be dysfunctional.

Lack of Reciprocity: If relationships within the group are one-sided, it's a sign of toxicity.

Gaslighting & Manipulation in Friendships

Gaslighting is a form of psychological manipulation where a person makes you question your reality and self-worth. In toxic friendships, gaslighting can take various forms:

Dismissing your feelings by saying, "You're too sensitive."

Twisting facts to make you feel responsible for conflicts.

Denying past agreements or conversations to confuse and control.

Making you feel guilty for setting boundaries.

4.2 How to Distance Yourself Without Conflict

Once you identify a toxic friendship or group, the next step is to remove yourself from the negative dynamic without unnecessary confrontation.

Strategies for Setting Boundaries

Establishing firm boundaries can help reduce interactions with toxic individuals without creating hostility.

Limit Contact: Gradually reduce conversations and interactions instead of abrupt disengagement.

Be Assertive but Kind: Use direct and polite communication when addressing issues.

Avoid Drama: Refrain from engaging in arguments or justifying your choices.

Prioritize Self-Care: Spend time with supportive people and focus on personal well-being.

Ending Friendships with Dignity

If distancing yourself isn't enough, formally ending the friendship may be necessary.

Express Gratitude & Closure: Acknowledge any positive aspects before moving on.

Keep It Brief & Clear: Avoid lengthy explanations that may lead to further arguments.

Remain Firm: Once you decide to walk away, do not get drawn back in by guilt or manipulation.

<u>Handling Social Backlash & Loneliness</u>

Leaving a toxic social group can sometimes lead to temporary isolation. Here's how to cope:

Lean on Healthier Relationships: Strengthen bonds with positive individuals in your life.

Engage in New Activities: Join groups, hobbies, or communities that align with your values.

Focus on Personal Growth: Use solitude to reflect, heal, and improve your well-being.

4.3 Rebuilding Your Social Life After Letting Go

Once you remove toxicity from your life, rebuilding a healthier and more fulfilling social network becomes essential.

<u>Finding & Nurturing Healthier Friendships</u>

Surrounding yourself with genuine and supportive people can enrich your life and provide emotional security.

Seek Out Like-Minded Individuals: Engage in activities where people share your values and interests.

Invest in Meaningful Conversations: Build deeper connections by discussing shared passions and values.

Be a Good Friend: Offer kindness, trust, and reciprocity to create lasting bonds.

<u>The Role of Self-Awareness in Choosing the Right Social Circles</u>

Self-awareness helps in recognizing what type of friendships best align with your personality and life goals.

Assess Past Patterns: Reflect on previous friendships to identify red flags you may have ignored.

Set Personal Standards: Decide what qualities matter most in friendships and relationships.

Trust Your Intuition: If something feels off in a new friendship, pay attention to those instincts.

<u>How Solitude Can Be a Growth Opportunity</u>

Spending time alone allows for self-discovery and emotional healing.

Develop Independence: Being comfortable alone strengthens emotional resilience.

Clarify Personal Goals: Use solitude to reflect on your aspirations and values.

Cultivate Self-Love: Strengthen your confidence before re-entering social dynamics.

Conclusion: Prioritizing Emotional Well-Being in Social Circles

Identifying and protecting yourself from toxic social dynamics is crucial for emotional health and overall happiness. By recognizing toxic relationships, setting boundaries, and surrounding yourself with positive influences, you create a support system that nurtures growth and well-being. Remember, friendships should bring joy, not emotional turmoil—choose wisely and prioritize relationships that align with your values.

CHAPTER TWENTY-FIVE

CRAFTING A MEANINGFUL & BALANCED SOCIAL LIFE

5.1 The Art of Meaningful Friendships

Friendships are a fundamental aspect of human life, providing emotional support, joy, and personal growth. However, not all friendships are created equal. A meaningful friendship is one where both individuals experience mutual respect, understanding, and growth.

<u>How to Recognize and Cultivate Deep, Fulfilling Relationships</u>

Emotional Reciprocity: A strong friendship involves mutual support rather than one-sided emotional labor.

Aligned Values and Interests: Shared core beliefs and passions foster stronger bonds.

Trust and Reliability: Knowing you can count on someone strengthens emotional security.

Communication and Vulnerability: Open and honest conversations create deeper connections.

<u>The Importance of Emotional Reciprocity</u>

A meaningful friendship is a two-way street. Here are ways to ensure reciprocity:

Show up consistently: Be there for friends during both good and difficult times.

Listen actively: Practice empathy and avoid dominating conversations.

Express gratitude: Acknowledge and appreciate friends for their presence and contributions.

<u>How to Be a Good Friend Without Losing Yourself</u>

Maintaining friendships should not come at the cost of personal well-being. Here's how to strike a balance:

Set boundaries: Know when to say no without guilt.

Prioritize self-care: A healthy friendship allows space for personal growth.

Avoid people-pleasing: Genuine friendships should not require constant validation-seeking.

5.2 The Power of Selective Socializing

Quality over quantity is key when building a balanced social life. Selective socializing helps individuals avoid toxic relationships while nurturing authentic connections.

<u>How to Balance Social Engagement with Personal Well-Being</u>

Assess energy levels: Identify how much social interaction aligns with your emotional bandwidth.

Choose social settings wisely: Engage in gatherings that provide meaningful interactions rather than obligatory participation.

Mix solitude with socializing: Alone time is essential for self-reflection and growth.

<u>Choosing People Who Align with Your Values and Goals</u>

Not everyone you meet deserves a place in your inner circle. Select friends who:

Uplift and inspire: Choose people who encourage your dreams and personal growth.

Respect your individuality: Surround yourself with those who celebrate your uniqueness.

Offer genuine support: Seek friendships based on authenticity, not convenience.

<u>The Importance of Solitude in Personal Growth</u>

Solitude is often mistaken for loneliness, but it plays a crucial role in self-awareness and personal development.

Strengthens independence: Helps you rely on yourself for happiness.

Encourages self-reflection: Provides clarity on personal goals and values.

Reduces social fatigue: Offers a break from external pressures and expectations.

5.3 Building a Social Life That Aligns with Your Purpose

A well-balanced social life is intentional. It should complement personal aspirations, values, and overall life goals.

Understanding That Not Every Connection Should Be Nurtured

Some relationships serve a short-term purpose and naturally fade away. Learning to let go is vital.

Identify relationships that no longer serve you: Some friendships are built on past circumstances rather than present values.

Recognize when to move on: If a relationship drains your energy rather than uplifts you, it might be time to distance yourself.

Accept that social circles evolve: Life changes, and so do friendships. It's okay to outgrow relationships.

How to Maintain a Healthy Balance Between Social and Personal Life

Schedule social interactions mindfully: Avoid overcommitting to social events at the expense of personal downtime.

Set digital boundaries: Social media can create the illusion of connection without genuine interaction.

Value quality interactions over frequency: Meaningful conversations are more valuable than frequent but superficial interactions.

Recognizing That Friendships and Networks Should Serve Mutual Growth

A social life should not be about mere socializing; it should enrich personal and professional development.

Find communities that align with your aspirations: Join groups and events related to your passions.

Invest in mutually beneficial relationships: Seek friendships where both parties contribute equally.

Adapt and evolve: Stay open to new relationships that align with evolving personal and professional goals.

Conclusion: Creating a Social Life That Adds Value

A meaningful and balanced social life requires effort, self-awareness, and intentionality. By choosing relationships that align with personal values, prioritizing quality over quantity, and maintaining a balance between solitude and socializing, individuals can create an enriching social environment that fosters growth, happiness, and fulfillment.

The ultimate goal is to build a social life that supports and enhances well-being rather than depleting it. The key lies in making intentional choices about whom to surround oneself with and how to engage in relationships in a way that adds lasting value.

Career & Professional Growth: Spotting Red Flags in Work & Leadership

CHAPTER TWENTY-SIX

UNDERSTANDING RED FLAGS IN CAREER GROWTH & LEADERSHIP

The Role of Red Flags in Professional Success

<u>Why Identifying Red Flags Matters</u>

Red flags in career growth and leadership are often warning signs of potential professional pitfalls, unethical practices, or toxic environments. These indicators can be subtle, overlooked, or even normalized in corporate culture. However, recognizing them early can be the difference between a thriving career and prolonged professional stagnation.

Many professionals ignore these warning signs due to emotional investment, financial security concerns, or an overarching belief in an organization's or leader's potential to change. However, failing to acknowledge these red flags can lead to burnout, career regression, or even reputational damage. Successful professionals have the ability to critically evaluate their work environment and leadership, ensuring that their growth trajectory aligns with their long-term aspirations.

<u>The Cost of Ignoring Red Flags</u>

Ignoring workplace red flags can have serious consequences, including:

Career Stagnation: Being stuck in an environment that does not provide growth opportunities can lead to skill decay and professional dissatisfaction.

Emotional & Mental Health Toll: Working in toxic environments can lead to stress, anxiety, and burnout.

Ethical Compromise: Being part of an organization that engages in unethical practices may eventually force professionals to choose between their values and their paycheck.

Missed Opportunities: Staying in a job with a toxic leader or unclear growth path can prevent professionals from seeking better opportunities elsewhere.

The key to long-term success lies in identifying these signs early and making informed career decisions that support both professional and personal well-being.

<u>The Fraud Examiner's Lens on Professional Growth</u>

As a fraud examiner, the ability to detect deception, analyze risks, and assess credibility is crucial. These same principles can be applied to professional growth and leadership assessment. Fraud detection techniques rely on recognizing patterns of misrepresentation, false promises, and inconsistencies—similar patterns appear in workplaces that stifle career growth or are led by ineffective leadership.

Due Diligence on Employers & Leaders: Just as fraud examiners scrutinize financial records and transactions, professionals should investigate company culture, leadership, and growth opportunities before accepting roles.

Identifying Inconsistencies in Leadership Promises: A leader who consistently makes promises but fails to deliver is similar to a company manipulating financial statements—it indicates a lack of integrity.

Analyzing Behavioral Patterns: Fraudsters often use manipulation and deception to gain trust. Similarly, toxic leaders or companies use persuasion tactics to prevent employees from recognizing workplace toxicity.

Understanding these methods allows professionals to navigate their careers with greater clarity, strategy, and resilience.

<u>Why Professionals Overlook Red Flags</u>

Despite clear warning signs, many professionals struggle to acknowledge red flags in their careers. The reasons vary, but some common ones include:

Financial Security & Stability:Fear of financial instability often forces professionals to tolerate toxic environments.The comfort of a steady paycheck can outweigh concerns about career stagnation.

Emotional Investment:Long tenure at an organization or deep relationships with colleagues can create a false sense of loyalty.Employees often hold on to the hope that things will improve despite evidence to the contrary.

Cognitive Bias & Rationalization:Professionals convince themselves that all workplaces have problems.The sunk cost fallacy makes it difficult to walk away from a company where years of effort have already been invested.

Fear of Change:The uncertainty of switching jobs or industries can be overwhelming.Doubts about one's own abilities may make staying in a familiar, albeit flawed, environment seem like the safer option.

<u>The Link Between Career Red Flags & Leadership Failures</u>

A major source of workplace red flags comes from poor leadership. Leadership plays a defining role in shaping company culture, career growth opportunities, and employee satisfaction. When leadership is ineffective, disengaged, or unethical, it creates systemic issues that trickle down into daily operations and long-term professional prospects.

<u>Common Leadership Red Flags</u>

Lack of Vision & Direction:Leaders who cannot articulate clear goals for the company or team.Rapidly shifting priorities that create confusion and inefficiency.

Poor Communication & Transparency:Important decisions are made without consulting or informing employees.Employees feel left in the dark about key business operations or strategy changes.

Unethical Behavior & Dishonesty:Leadership that bends or breaks rules to meet targets.Leaders who make false promises regarding promotions, raises, or company direction.

Micromanagement & Lack of Trust:Employees feel restricted and unable to make independent decisions. Leadership fails to delegate effectively, leading to frustration and stagnation.

Ignoring Employee Growth & Well-being:No investment in employee training, mentorship, or career development.Lack of concern for employee mental health, work-life balance, or well-being.

<u>Red Flags as a Tool for Career Growth</u>

Instead of viewing red flags purely as warnings, professionals can use them as guidance tools. Recognizing and responding to these signals can help in making better career decisions, choosing the right employers, and positioning oneself for long-term success.

Turning Red Flags into Career Growth Opportunities

Assessing a Workplace Before Accepting a Job:Research company culture through reviews, networking, and interviews.Ask direct questions about leadership, career progression, and company values.

Strategically Navigating a Toxic Work Environment:Set clear professional boundaries to mitigate workplace toxicity.Create an exit strategy while upskilling and networking for better opportunities.

Developing Leadership Awareness:Seek mentorship from ethical, competent leaders.Learn to recognize leadership styles that support or hinder professional development.

Conclusion: The Power of Awareness in Career Success

The ability to identify, analyze, and respond to career red flags is a critical skill for professionals seeking long-term success. Much like fraud examiners rely on investigative techniques to uncover deception, professionals must sharpen their ability to spot leadership and workplace red flags to protect their careers.

By fostering self-awareness, conducting due diligence, and making informed career decisions, individuals can ensure that their career growth remains ethical, strategic, and aligned with their professional aspirations. Ultimately, spotting and responding to red flags is not just about avoiding negative experiences—it's about positioning oneself for sustainable success and leadership in any industry.

CHAPTER TWENTY-SEVEN

WORKPLACE RED FLAGS: RECOGNIZING A TOXIC WORK ENVIRONMENT

Introduction

A toxic work environment can significantly hinder productivity, employee satisfaction, and overall career growth. Many professionals find themselves in unhealthy workplaces due to financial security concerns, lack of awareness, or the hope that things will improve. Recognizing red flags early is essential to making informed career decisions and protecting one's mental and emotional well-being. This section will explore the key indicators of a toxic work environment, their impact, and strategies for navigating or exiting such situations.

1. Organizational Red Flags

<u>High Employee Turnover</u>

A revolving door of employees often signals deep-rooted organizational problems. Companies with high turnover rates may suffer from poor leadership, lack of career growth opportunities, or an unhealthy work culture. Employees frequently leaving an organization could indicate:

Unfulfilled promises regarding promotions or salary increases.

An unsupportive work environment where employees feel undervalued.

Constant restructuring or layoffs creating job insecurity.

<u>Lack of Transparency</u>

Transparency is key to building trust between employees and management. Warning signs of a lack of transparency include:

Unclear or misleading communication about company performance.

Secretive leadership that withholds key information from employees.

Decisions made without proper explanation, leading to confusion and distrust.

<u>Unclear Vision and Direction</u>

Organizations without a clear mission or defined goals often struggle with inefficiency and instability. Employees may feel lost or unmotivated when:

Goals shift frequently without justification.

Leadership fails to provide a structured roadmap for growth.

Employees receive mixed messages about priorities and expectations.

2. Cultural Red Flags

<u>Office Politics and Favoritism</u>

Toxic workplaces are often characterized by office politics, favoritism, and cliques that create divisions among employees. Common warning signs include:

Promotions and opportunities are given based on personal relationships rather than merit.

A culture where backstabbing and gossip thrive.

Employees feel excluded or undervalued due to unfair biases.

<u>Workplace Bullying and Harassment</u>

A healthy workplace should be free from intimidation, bullying, or harassment. Signs of a hostile work culture include:

Employees facing verbal abuse, humiliation, or unreasonable criticism.

Leaders who tolerate or ignore workplace harassment complaints.

A lack of policies or enforcement to protect employees from mistreatment.

<u>Work-Life Imbalance</u>

Organizations that do not prioritize employee well-being can cause burnout and stress. Red flags include:

Expecting employees to be available 24/7 or regularly work excessive hours.

A culture where taking vacations or sick leave is frowned upon.

Employees feeling guilty or anxious about maintaining a work-life balance.

3. Operational Red Flags

<u>Unethical Business Practices</u>

A company's integrity directly impacts employee trust and long-term stability. Indicators of unethical practices include:

Manipulating financial data or engaging in fraudulent activities.

Encouraging employees to bend rules to meet business goals.

Retaliating against whistleblowers who expose unethical behavior.

<u>Lack of Employee Development and Growth</u>

Organizations that do not invest in employee development may struggle with low morale and high turnover. Warning signs include:

Lack of training programs or mentorship opportunities.

Employees stuck in the same roles without clear growth paths.

Leaders who discourage innovation or new ideas.

Unrealistic Expectations and Constant Crisis Mode

Workplaces that demand excessive work without support create a toxic cycle of stress and burnout. Indicators include:

Employees expected to meet unrealistic deadlines without proper resources.

A culture where constant firefighting replaces strategic planning.

Employees feeling pressured to prioritize work over personal well-being.

4. Leadership Red Flags

<u>Poor Communication and Lack of Accountability</u>

Leaders who fail to communicate effectively create confusion and frustration among employees. Warning signs include:

Vague instructions or frequent last-minute changes.

Leaders who refuse to accept responsibility for failures.

A blame culture where employees are held accountable for leadership mistakes.

<u>Micromanagement or Absentee Leadership</u>

A toxic workplace can suffer from two extremes: micromanagement or disengaged leadership. Indicators include:

Leaders who overly control every aspect of an employee's work.

Managers who fail to provide guidance, support, or constructive feedback.

Employees feeling either suffocated or abandoned by leadership.

<u>Ignoring Employee Well-being</u>

A company's treatment of its employees reflects its values. Red flags include:

Leaders dismissing mental health concerns or failing to provide adequate resources.

A culture where expressing workplace concerns leads to punishment or retaliation.

Employees consistently feeling undervalued, unsupported, or expendable.

5. Strategies for Handling a Toxic Workplace

<u>Assessing the Situation</u>

Before making any career moves, professionals should evaluate whether the workplace issues are temporary or systemic. Questions to consider:

Is the toxicity widespread or limited to specific individuals?

Have past employees raised similar concerns?

Is there an opportunity to improve the situation through internal discussions?

<u>Setting Boundaries</u>

Employees can protect themselves from toxic environments by:

Defining work-life boundaries and sticking to them.

Avoiding unnecessary involvement in office politics or conflicts.

Communicating clearly and professionally to avoid misinterpretations.

<u>Exploring Exit Strategies</u>

When toxicity persists, preparing to transition to a better work environment is essential. Steps include:

Updating resumes and networking for new opportunities.

Seeking mentorship or career counseling to explore options.

Ensuring financial stability before resigning.

<u>Speaking Up When Necessary</u>

If employees choose to stay, they may attempt to address workplace issues by:

Documenting incidents of toxicity as evidence.

Reporting concerns to HR or higher management.

Proposing constructive solutions to create a healthier work culture.

Conclusion

A toxic workplace can drain employees emotionally, mentally, and professionally. Recognizing red flags early empowers individuals to make informed decisions about their careers. While some workplace issues can be addressed, others require a strategic exit. Employees should prioritize environments that foster respect, integrity, and growth. By staying vigilant and proactive, professionals can build fulfilling careers free from toxicity and undue stress.

CHAPTER TWENTY-EIGHT

Leadership Red Flags: Spotting Bad Bosses & Misguided Mentors

Introduction

Leadership plays a critical role in shaping workplace culture, employee satisfaction, and career development. Good leaders inspire, guide, and nurture talent, whereas bad leaders can create toxicity, hinder growth, and damage morale. Recognizing red flags in leadership early can help professionals make informed decisions about their workplace and career trajectory. This section will explore common leadership red flags, their impact, and how to navigate situations involving ineffective or toxic leaders.

1. Identifying Toxic Leadership Traits

Micromanagement and Lack of Trust

Micromanagers create an oppressive work environment by excessively controlling employees' tasks and decisions. Warning signs include:

Constantly checking in on minor details without allowing autonomy.

Overriding employee decisions without justification.

Discouraging independent thinking and creativity.

Lack of Transparency and Dishonesty

Leaders who fail to communicate openly breed confusion and distrust. Common indicators include:

Providing vague or misleading information about company goals and policies.

Avoiding difficult conversations and withholding important updates.

Making false promises regarding promotions, salary increases, or job security.

<u>Inconsistent Decision-Making</u>

Unpredictable leadership creates instability in the workplace. Signs of erratic leadership include:

Frequently changing priorities without clear reasoning.

Favoritism in decision-making, treating employees unequally.

A lack of accountability when mistakes are made.

<u>Credit-Stealing and Blame-Shifting</u>

Toxic leaders often take credit for team achievements while blaming employees for failures. Warning signs include:

Ignoring contributions of subordinates in meetings and reports.

Publicly blaming employees for mistakes rather than taking accountability.

Failing to recognize or reward hard work.

2. Recognizing Manipulative and Self-Serving Leaders

<u>Narcissistic and Egotistical Behavior</u>

Some leaders prioritize their own success over the well-being of their employees. Common narcissistic tendencies include:

A constant need for admiration and validation.

Dismissing feedback or criticism as personal attacks.

Making decisions that serve their personal interests rather than the team's.

<u>Gaslighting and Psychological Manipulation</u>

Manipulative leaders distort reality to maintain control over employees. Signs include:

Dismissing legitimate concerns by making employees doubt their own judgment.

Shifting blame to subordinates to evade responsibility.

Withholding information to keep employees in a state of uncertainty.

<u>Encouraging Unethical Behavior</u>

Some leaders pressure employees into unethical actions for personal or company gain. Red flags include:

Asking employees to manipulate data, mislead clients, or bend company policies.

Prioritizing short-term profits over ethical business practices.

Retaliating against employees who raise ethical concerns.

3. The Fake Mentor: When Guidance Goes Wrong

<u>Hindering Employee Growth</u>

A good mentor fosters career development, but a misguided mentor can stifle progress. Red flags include:

Discouraging employees from pursuing new opportunities or learning new skills.

Offering advice that prioritizes their own interests rather than the employee's growth.

Failing to provide constructive feedback or career guidance.

<u>Favoritism and Unfair Treatment</u>

A mentor should be objective and supportive of all team members. Warning signs of biased mentorship include:

Only investing time and resources in select employees while neglecting others.

Providing opportunities based on personal relationships rather than merit.

Setting different performance expectations for different team members.

<u>Mentorship as a Power Play</u>

Some leaders use mentorship to exert control rather than offer genuine support. Common manipulative tactics include:

Using mentorship as a way to micromanage employees rather than empower them.

Making mentees overly dependent on their guidance, limiting independence.

Withholding critical knowledge to maintain superiority over employees.

4. The Impact of Poor Leadership on Employees

<u>Decline in Morale and Motivation</u>

Employees subjected to bad leadership often experience burnout and disengagement. Consequences include:

Increased absenteeism due to workplace stress.

A decline in enthusiasm and commitment to the job.

A toxic workplace culture where employees feel undervalued.

<u>Stagnation in Career Growth</u>

Ineffective leadership can hinder an employee's professional development. Effects include:

Limited opportunities for promotions or skill-building.

A lack of mentorship or coaching for career advancement.

Feeling stuck in a position without prospects for growth.

<u>Negative Effects on Mental and Emotional Well-Being</u>

Toxic leaders create an environment that takes a toll on employees' health. Common impacts include:

Anxiety and stress resulting from unrealistic expectations.

Loss of confidence due to constant criticism or gaslighting.

Increased risk of burnout and job dissatisfaction.

5. Strategies for Navigating Toxic Leadership

<u>Assessing the Work Environment</u>

Before taking any action, employees should evaluate the severity of the leadership issues. Key questions to consider:

Are the leadership problems isolated or part of a larger pattern?

Is there a way to address the concerns internally without repercussions?

Have others in the organization experienced similar challenges?

<u>Setting Boundaries and Protecting Yourself</u>

Employees can take proactive measures to mitigate the effects of poor leadership. Strategies include:

Maintaining professional boundaries to avoid being drawn into office politics.

Keeping detailed records of interactions and decisions for future reference.

Seeking peer support to validate concerns and share coping strategies.

<u>Seeking Alternative Support and Growth Opportunities</u>

If leadership issues persist, employees should explore ways to grow outside their immediate environment. Options include:

Finding mentorship from other experienced professionals within or outside the company.

Taking online courses or professional development programs to build new skills.

Expanding professional networks to identify potential career opportunities.

<u>Knowing When to Leave</u>

In some cases, the best solution is to exit a toxic work environment. Signs it's time to move on include:

No signs of improvement despite addressing concerns with management.

Persistent stress and anxiety affecting personal and professional well-being.

Better career opportunities available in organizations with healthier cultures.

Conclusion

Recognizing leadership red flags is crucial for maintaining a positive career trajectory. Poor leadership can stifle growth, reduce motivation, and create a toxic work environment. By staying vigilant, setting boundaries, and seeking mentorship from ethical leaders, professionals can safeguard their career and well-being. When leadership issues become unsolvable, knowing when to leave and pursue better opportunities can be the key to long-term success.

CHAPTER TWENTY-NINE

CAREER DECISION RED FLAGS: WHEN TO STAY, WHEN TO LEAVE

Introduction

Making career decisions is one of the most significant choices a professional can face. Deciding whether to stay in a job or move on is rarely black and white—there are multiple factors to consider. While every career has ups and downs, there are critical red flags that indicate when a job is no longer serving your personal and professional growth. Recognizing these warning signs early can prevent stagnation, burnout, and missed opportunities. This section will explore the key indicators that suggest whether you should stay or leave a job and provide strategies for making a well-informed decision.

1. Warning Signs That You Should Consider Leaving

<u>Lack of Career Growth and Development</u>

One of the clearest signs that it's time to move on is stagnation in your role. If you notice the following, it may be time to seek new opportunities:

No opportunities for skill development or promotions.

Your role has remained the same for years with no new challenges.

Management does not support professional growth through mentorship or training.

<u>Toxic Work Environment</u>

A toxic workplace can severely impact your mental health and job satisfaction. Warning signs include:

High turnover rates among employees.

Office politics, gossip, or bullying.

A culture of blame, where employees are constantly under scrutiny.

Unethical practices, such as dishonesty, discrimination, or favoritism.

<u>Lack of Recognition and Appreciation</u>

Feeling undervalued can lead to frustration and disengagement. If your efforts go unnoticed, consider whether:

Your hard work is consistently ignored.

Promotions and salary increases are given unfairly.

Your contributions are not acknowledged by leadership.

<u>Work-Life Imbalance</u>

Burnout is a major reason why professionals leave jobs. If your work is affecting your personal life negatively, take note of:

Consistently working overtime without additional compensation.

Expectations to be available 24/7, including nights and weekends.

Physical and mental health suffering due to stress and lack of rest.

<u>Uncertain Company Future</u>

A struggling company can put your job security at risk. Red flags include:

Frequent layoffs or budget cuts.

Declining revenue and lack of business growth.

Poor management decisions leading to financial instability.

<u>Compensation Issues</u>

While passion is important, fair compensation is crucial for job satisfaction. Signs that indicate it's time to move on:

Salary significantly below industry standards.

Consistently delayed or missing payments.

No raises or benefits despite increasing responsibilities.

<u>Lack of Alignment with Personal Goals and Values</u>

If your job no longer aligns with your career aspirations and values, ask yourself:

Does this role support my long-term goals?

Do I feel motivated and passionate about my work?

Am I compromising my ethics to stay in this job?

2. Signs That You Should Stay and Grow

<u>Opportunities for Advancement</u>

If your company provides a clear path for career progression, it may be worth staying. Consider:

Mentorship and training programs that support your development.

Potential promotions or lateral moves to expand your skill set.

A supportive leadership team that values employee growth.

<u>Healthy Work Culture and Team Support</u>

A positive work environment can outweigh minor job frustrations. Signs of a great workplace include:

Strong relationships with colleagues and managers.

Open communication and constructive feedback.

A culture of respect and inclusivity.

<u>Fair Compensation and Benefits</u>

If your salary and benefits package is competitive and meets your needs, staying may be the right choice. Key factors include:

Regular raises and performance-based bonuses.

Comprehensive health benefits and retirement plans.

Work-life balance initiatives like flexible work schedules.

<u>Challenging and Meaningful Work</u>

If your job continues to challenge and engage you, it can be rewarding to stay. Consider:

Opportunities to work on exciting projects.

A role that keeps you learning and growing.

Work that aligns with your passion and purpose.

<u>Good Leadership and Company Stability</u>

If your company is well-managed and financially stable, it can provide long-term career benefits. Look for:

Strong leadership that values employee input.

Transparent business strategies and decision-making.

A clear vision for the company's future.

3. How to Evaluate Your Situation Objectively

<u>Self-Reflection and Career Assessment</u>

Before making a decision, take time to reflect on:

Your career goals and whether your current job aligns with them.

The aspects of your job that you enjoy and those that frustrate you.

Whether you feel challenged and valued in your role.

<u>Talk to Trusted Mentors or Colleagues</u>

Seeking external perspectives can provide valuable insight. Discuss your concerns with:

A mentor or coach who can offer objective advice.

Colleagues who may have faced similar challenges.

Friends or family who understand your career aspirations.

<u>Conduct a Pros and Cons Analysis</u>

List the advantages and disadvantages of staying in your job. Consider factors such as:

Salary, benefits, and career growth opportunities.

Work-life balance and company culture.

The likelihood of long-term job satisfaction.

<u>Evaluate Job Market Conditions</u>

Before resigning, assess the job market for opportunities that align with your skills and goals. Research:

Industry demand for your role and expertise.

Potential salary increases in a new position.

Companies that offer better career growth.

4. Creating an Exit Strategy if You Decide to Leave

<u>Plan Your Transition</u>

If you decide to move on, ensure a smooth transition by:

Securing a new job before resigning (if possible).

Building financial stability to cover expenses during the transition.

Networking with industry professionals to explore opportunities.

<u>Resign Professionally</u>

Leaving on good terms is important for maintaining a positive reputation. Follow best practices such as:

Providing a formal resignation letter with adequate notice.

Expressing gratitude for the opportunities provided.

Assisting with knowledge transfer before leaving.

<u>Negotiate a Better Offer in Your Next Role</u>

Use your exit as an opportunity to secure better terms in your next job. Consider:

Negotiating a higher salary based on your experience.

Seeking additional benefits like remote work options or flexible hours.

Clarifying career growth opportunities before accepting an offer.

Conclusion

Deciding whether to stay in a job or move on is a crucial career decision that should be based on careful evaluation. Red flags such as lack of growth, toxic culture, and poor compensation indicate that it may be time to leave. However, if the job provides opportunities for advancement, fair compensation, and a positive work environment, staying and growing within the company may be the right choice. By analyzing your situation objectively and planning your next steps strategically, you can make career decisions that support both your professional and personal success.

CHAPTER THIRTY

THRIVING BEYOND RED FLAGS: BUILDING A RESILIENT CAREER

Introduction

In every career, professionals will encounter workplace red flags—signs of toxic leadership, stagnant growth, or unethical practices. However, recognizing these signs is only half the battle. The key to long-term success is learning how to navigate these challenges, build resilience, and thrive in the face of adversity. A resilient career is one that not only survives setbacks but continues to grow and evolve despite obstacles.

This section will explore strategies for overcoming career setbacks, leveraging difficult experiences for growth, and fostering long-term professional resilience.

1. Understanding Career Resilience

Career resilience is the ability to adapt, recover, and thrive in the face of challenges. Resilient professionals demonstrate:

Adaptability: The ability to pivot and embrace change.

Emotional Intelligence: Managing emotions effectively in professional settings.

Continuous Learning: A commitment to growth despite obstacles.

Networking and Support Systems: Leveraging professional relationships for guidance and opportunities.

Self-Advocacy: Recognizing one's value and seeking environments that support growth.

2. Developing a Resilient Mindset

A strong mindset is the foundation of career resilience. Key strategies include:

<u>Shifting Perspectives on Setbacks</u>

Viewing career challenges as opportunities for growth rather than failures.

Learning from setbacks by assessing what went wrong and how to improve.

Recognizing that setbacks do not define long-term career potential.

<u>Building Emotional Resilience</u>

Managing workplace stress through mindfulness and self-care.

Setting healthy boundaries to prevent burnout.

Practicing gratitude and focusing on positive aspects of work life.

<u>Maintaining Confidence and Self-Worth</u>

Not allowing toxic workplaces or negative experiences to diminish self-esteem.

Regularly reflecting on accomplishments and strengths.

Surrounding oneself with supportive mentors and peers.

3. Turning Red Flags into Growth Opportunities

Every challenge presents an opportunity to learn. Instead of being discouraged by workplace red flags, use them as learning experiences.

<u>Extracting Lessons from Negative Experiences</u>

Identifying what worked and what didn't in past job roles.

Recognizing early warning signs to make better future career decisions.

Strengthening problem-solving skills by navigating difficult situations.

<u>Using Adversity to Build Career Strength</u>

Developing resilience by overcoming workplace challenges.

Improving conflict resolution skills when dealing with difficult colleagues or managers.

Strengthening leadership qualities by learning from poor leadership examples.

4. Proactively Building a Resilient Career Path

Rather than reacting to problems, professionals should proactively shape their careers to minimize setbacks.

<u>Prioritizing Skill Development and Lifelong Learning</u>

Continuously upgrading skills to remain competitive in the job market.

Seeking additional certifications, training, or educational opportunities.

Staying updated with industry trends and emerging technologies.

<u>Networking and Building Strong Professional Relationships</u>

Connecting with mentors who can provide guidance and support.

Engaging in industry events, online communities, and professional organizations.

Leveraging relationships for job opportunities and career advancement.

<u>Seeking Positive Work Environments</u>

Researching company culture before accepting job offers.

Prioritizing organizations that offer strong leadership, transparency, and growth opportunities.

Advocating for oneself in negotiations regarding salary, responsibilities, and career development.

5. Bouncing Back from Career Setbacks

Even with resilience, setbacks will occur. Knowing how to recover is crucial for long-term career success.

<u>Recovering from Job Loss or Layoffs</u>

Maintaining financial preparedness to handle unexpected job loss.

Strategically job searching rather than accepting the first opportunity out of desperation.

Using the time to upskill, network, and explore new career paths.

<u>Overcoming Toxic Work Experiences</u>

Seeking therapy or coaching to process workplace trauma.

Reframing the experience as a stepping stone rather than a failure.

Using past experiences to make more informed career decisions moving forward.

<u>Rebuilding Confidence After Career Disruptions</u>

Setting small, achievable goals to regain career momentum.

Celebrating personal and professional achievements along the way.

Practicing self-compassion and patience in the recovery process.

Conclusion

Building a resilient career requires recognizing red flags, learning from challenges, and proactively shaping one's professional path. While obstacles are inevitable, professionals who cultivate adaptability, emotional intelligence, and a strong support network will not only survive setbacks but thrive beyond them. By fostering a mindset of continuous growth and strategic decision-making, anyone can turn adversity into opportunity and build a fulfilling, resilient career.

Financial Health & Stability: Due Diligence for Your Wallet and Your Future

CHAPTER THIRTY-ONE

UNDERSTANDING FINANCIAL HEALTH

Introduction

Financial health is the foundation of a stable and secure life. Just as physical health requires regular check-ups, good habits, and discipline, financial health also demands constant monitoring, strategic planning, and responsible decision-making.

A financially healthy person is not necessarily the wealthiest but is someone who has control over their finances, can meet financial obligations without stress, and is prepared for unexpected expenses. In this section, we will explore what financial health means, how to assess your own financial situation, and how psychology influences financial behavior.

1. Defining Financial Health & Stability

<u>What Constitutes Financial Health?</u>

Financial health is a holistic measure of your financial well-being, which includes:

Having enough income to cover expenses comfortably.

Maintaining a balanced budget without excessive debt.

Saving consistently for future needs and emergencies.

Investing wisely to build long-term wealth.

Ensuring financial security against risks (e.g., job loss, medical emergencies).

The goal of financial health is not just to survive but to thrive—having the financial freedom to make life choices without constant worry about money.

<u>Wealth vs. Financial Stability</u>

People often confuse financial stability with wealth. Wealth refers to the total value of assets owned, while financial stability is about maintaining a balance between income, expenses, savings, and debt to ensure consistent financial security.

For example, a person earning millions but spending recklessly with no savings or investments is financially unhealthy. Meanwhile, someone with a moderate income but strong financial discipline may be much more financially stable.

<u>The Role of Financial Well-being in Mental and Physical Health</u>

Financial stress is a leading cause of anxiety and depression. Studies have shown that people struggling with money often experience:

Sleep disturbances

Higher levels of stress hormones

Poor decision-making due to anxiety

Achieving financial stability not only improves your economic situation but also contributes to overall well-being, reducing stress and increasing confidence in your future.

2. Assessing Your Financial Health

<u>Key Indicators of Financial Health</u>

How do you know if you are financially healthy? Here are five key indicators:

Net Worth – The total value of your assets minus liabilities (debts).

Formula: Net Worth = Assets - Liabilities

A positive and growing net worth over time indicates financial health.

Liquidity Ratio – Your ability to cover short-term expenses with liquid assets (cash, savings, etc.).

A high liquidity ratio means you are prepared for unexpected expenses.

Savings Rate – The percentage of income you save every month.Recommended: Save at least 20-30% of your income.

Debt-to-Income Ratio – Measures how much of your income goes toward debt payments.

Healthy Range: Keep it below 30-35% of your income.

Financial Security Index – A self-assessment of how secure you feel about your finances.

Do you have enough savings to cover 6-12 months of expenses?

Can you handle a financial emergency without borrowing money?

<u>How to Perform a Personal Financial Audit</u>

Conducting a financial audit helps you assess your financial strengths and weaknesses. Steps to perform one:

List Your Income Sources – Include salary, side hustles, passive income, etc.

Record Monthly Expenses – Break them into fixed (rent, utilities) and variable (entertainment, shopping).

Calculate Your Savings & Investments – Track where your money is going.

Review Your Debt – Note outstanding loans, interest rates, and repayment terms.

Evaluate Your Financial Goals – Are you meeting your short- and long-term financial targets?

By performing a financial audit every six months, you can identify areas for improvement and track progress toward financial stability.

<u>Signs of Financial Distress vs. Financial Security</u>

? Financial Distress Warning Signs:

Living paycheck to paycheck.

Struggling to pay bills on time.

Carrying high-interest credit card debt.

No emergency savings or retirement plan.

? Signs of Financial Security:

Monthly expenses are covered comfortably.

Savings and investments grow consistently.

Debt is well-managed and decreasing.

Confidence in handling unexpected financial setbacks.

3. The Psychology of Money

<u>Understanding Spending Habits & Financial Behaviors</u>

Many financial problems stem from psychological patterns rather than lack of income. Your financial habits are often shaped by childhood experiences, social influences, and emotional triggers.

Common Financial Personality Types

The Saver – Prioritizes savings but may fear spending too much.

The Spender – Enjoys instant gratification but may struggle with saving.

The Investor – Focuses on growing wealth strategically.

The Avoider – Ignores financial issues due to anxiety or lack of knowledge.

Understanding your financial personality can help you make better money decisions.

<u>The Impact of Emotions on Financial Decisions</u>

Fear & Anxiety – Can lead to avoiding investment opportunities or hoarding cash instead of making strategic decisions.

Impulse Buying – Emotional spending often results from stress, social pressure, or advertising influences.

Overconfidence Bias – Leads to taking excessive financial risks without proper research.

Overcoming Financial Anxiety & Self-Sabotage

If financial stress is overwhelming, take the following steps:

✓ Educate Yourself – Read books, take finance courses, and seek professional advice.

✓ Create a Plan – Structure your financial goals with clear steps.

✓ Automate Finances – Set up automatic transfers for savings, bill payments, and investments.

✓ Build a Support System – Discuss financial goals with trusted friends, mentors, or financial advisors.

Conclusion

Understanding financial health is the first step toward financial freedom. It's not just about earning more but also about managing money wisely, making informed financial decisions, and cultivating a mindset that supports long-term stability.

? Key Takeaways:

Financial health is a balance of income, expenses, savings, and debt.

Conducting regular financial audits helps track progress and address weaknesses.

Financial behaviors are influenced by emotions, habits, and mindset.

Developing strong financial habits leads to long-term security and peace of mind.

By mastering financial health, you are setting the foundation for a financially secure and stress-free future. In the next section, we will explore Due Diligence in Financial Decision-Making, where we discuss how to analyze financial opportunities and protect yourself from common financial pitfalls

CHAPTER THIRTY-TWO

Due Diligence in Financial Decision-Making

Introduction

Financial decision-making is not just about earning and spending—it's about making informed, calculated choices that protect and grow your wealth. Due diligence is the process of thoroughly researching financial opportunities, evaluating risks, and identifying red flags before making any major financial commitments.

In this section, we will explore how to apply due diligence to personal finances, avoid common financial scams, assess investments wisely, and manage debt responsibly.

1. Financial Red Flags to Watch Out For

The Importance of Due Diligence in Personal Finance

Due diligence is a concept widely used in the corporate and investment world, but it is equally important for personal finances. It involves:

✓ Conducting thorough research before financial commitments.

✓ Understanding the risks and benefits of financial decisions.

✓ Identifying and avoiding scams and misleading financial products.

✓ Ensuring financial stability by making well-informed choices.

Common Financial Scams & Frauds

Fraudulent schemes prey on financial ignorance and emotional decision-making. Some of the most common financial scams include:

? Ponzi Schemes – Promises of high returns with little or no risk, where new investors' money is used to pay earlier investors. (Red Flag: Unrealistic returns, no clear business model.)

? Pyramid Schemes – Requires recruitment of members to earn profits rather than selling a real product or service. (Red Flag: Earnings come from recruitment, not actual sales.)

? Phishing Scams – Fake emails or calls claiming to be from banks, tax authorities, or credit card companies, attempting to steal sensitive information. (Red Flag: Urgent requests for personal or financial data.)

? Get-Rich-Quick Schemes – Any investment that guarantees high returns with little or no effort. (Red Flag: Lack of regulatory approvals, exaggerated earnings.)

? Insurance & Loan Frauds – Hidden clauses, misrepresentation of terms, and extremely high interest rates. (Red Flag: Unclear policies, pressure tactics.)

? How to Protect Yourself:

Always verify the credentials of financial institutions.

Never share sensitive financial information unless necessary.

Be skeptical of unsolicited investment offers.

Read contracts and fine print carefully before signing.

2. Due Diligence on Investments

<u>How to Assess Investment Opportunities</u>

Investments can be a great way to build wealth, but they come with risks. Conducting due diligence on investment options ensures that you're not making decisions based on hype or misleading information.

Key Steps for Investment Due Diligence

✓ Understand the Business Model – What does the company or asset actually do? How does it generate revenue?

✓ Evaluate the Financial Health – Review financial statements, earnings reports, and debt levels.

✓ Assess Risk vs. Return – Higher returns often mean higher risk. Are you comfortable with the potential downside?

✓ Check Regulatory Approvals – Is the investment legally registered with regulatory bodies (e.g., SEC, SEBI)?

✓ Research Market Trends – What are industry experts saying? Are there red flags in the market?

<u>Red Flags in Investment Opportunities</u>

? Guaranteed High Returns – If an investment promises high returns with low risk, it's likely a scam.

? No Transparency – If you cannot understand how the investment works, avoid it.

? Lack of Liquidity – Investments that do not allow easy withdrawal should be approached with caution.

? Pressure to Invest Quickly – Scammers create urgency to force impulsive decisions.

<u>Understanding Financial Statements & Red Flags</u>

If you're considering investing in a business, stock, or fund, reviewing financial statements is crucial. Key areas to check:

Income Statement: Look for consistent revenue growth and stable profitability.

Balance Sheet: Check for manageable debt levels and strong asset base.

Cash Flow Statement: Positive cash flow indicates a healthy business, while negative cash flow can signal trouble.

? Pro Tip: Avoid companies with high debt, inconsistent profits, or negative cash flows for prolonged periods.

3. Smart Borrowing & Credit Management

<u>When to Take Loans & When to Avoid Them</u>

Loans can be useful tools if used wisely, but borrowing without due diligence can lead to financial stress.

? Good Reasons to Take a Loan:

Buying a home (mortgage).

Investing in education or skill-building.

Starting or expanding a business.

? Bad Reasons to Take a Loan:

Funding luxury purchases (cars, vacations).

Paying off other debts (unless through refinancing at lower rates).

Impulse spending.

<u>Understanding Credit Scores & How to Improve Them</u>

A good credit score (700+) makes borrowing easier and cheaper.

Factors Affecting Credit Scores:

Payment History (35%) – Always pay bills on time.

Credit Utilization (30%) – Keep credit card usage below 30% of the limit.

Credit History Length (15%) – Older accounts improve scores.

Types of Credit (10%) – A mix of credit (loans, credit cards) is beneficial.

New Credit Inquiries (10%) – Avoid multiple hard inquiries within a short period.

? How to Improve Credit Score:

✓ Pay off debts on time.

✓ Reduce credit card utilization.

✓ Check credit reports for errors.

✓ Avoid applying for multiple loans at once.

4. Debt Traps & How to Avoid Them

<u>Understanding High-Interest Debt</u>

High-interest loans and revolving credit can drain financial resources quickly.

? Credit Card Debt – Interest rates can be 30-40% annually if balances aren't cleared monthly.

? Payday Loans – Extremely high-interest short-term loans that trap borrowers in cycles of debt.

? Buy Now, Pay Later (BNPL) Traps – These can accumulate into large debts if mismanaged.

<u>Strategies for Managing & Reducing Debt</u>

✓ Prioritize High-Interest Debt – Pay off high-interest loans first (Avalanche Method).

✓ Debt Snowball Approach – Pay off the smallest debts first to build momentum.

✓ Consolidate Debt – Refinancing loans at lower interest rates can save money.

✓ Negotiate with Lenders – Banks sometimes offer lower interest rates to responsible borrowers.

? Pro Tip: Always read the loan agreement carefully and check for hidden fees, penalties, and prepayment clauses.

5. Building a Financial Safety Net

<u>The Role of Emergency Funds</u>

An emergency fund acts as financial insurance, covering unexpected expenses like medical emergencies, job loss, or urgent repairs.

✓ How Much to Save? – Aim for 6-12 months' worth of living expenses.

✓ Where to Keep It? – A high-yield savings account for easy access.

✓ How to Build It? – Automate savings, cut unnecessary expenses, and redirect bonuses.

Insurance: A Critical Part of Due Diligence

Many people ignore insurance until it's too late. Proper due diligence ensures you choose the right policies.

Essential Insurance Types:

✓ Health Insurance – Covers medical emergencies.

✓ Life Insurance – Protects family members in case of an untimely death.

✓ Disability Insurance – Provides income in case of injury.

✓ Liability Insurance – Protects against legal claims.

Conclusion

Due diligence in financial decision-making is crucial for avoiding financial pitfalls, making smart investments, and ensuring long-term financial security.

? Key Takeaways:

Always verify financial opportunities before committing.

Watch for investment red flags like unrealistic returns or lack of transparency.

Use credit responsibly and improve your credit score to lower borrowing costs.

Avoid debt traps and prioritize paying off high-interest loans.

Build a financial safety net through emergency funds and insurance.

Applying due diligence to your financial life helps you make smarter, more secure choices, paving the way for long-term financial stability. ?

CHAPTER THIRTY-THREE

BUILDING FINANCIAL RESILIENCE

Introduction

Financial resilience is the ability to withstand and recover from financial hardships while maintaining stability and growth. Life is unpredictable—economic downturns, job loss, medical emergencies, or unexpected expenses can create financial stress. The key to long-term financial well-being is building resilience by strengthening your financial foundation, preparing for uncertainties, and developing sustainable wealth-building habits.

This section covers emergency funds, insurance strategies, diversification, and long-term financial planning to help you build resilience against financial setbacks.

1. Emergency Funds: Your Financial Safety Net

<u>Why an Emergency Fund is Essential</u>

An emergency fund is your first line of defense against financial shocks. Without one, you may be forced to borrow at high interest rates, dip into investments, or delay essential expenses.

Key Benefits:

✓ Covers unexpected expenses without disrupting your financial plan.

✓ Prevents unnecessary debt accumulation.

✓ Provides peace of mind and financial security.

<u>How Much Should You Save?</u>

A good rule of thumb is to have 6–12 months' worth of essential living expenses saved in an easily accessible account.

? Minimum Guidelines Based on Job Stability:

Stable Income (Government jobs, long-term employment): 3–6 months of expenses.

Unstable Income (Freelancers, entrepreneurs): 9–12 months of expenses.

High Dependents (Single earners, medical conditions): 12+ months of expenses.

<u>Where to Keep Your Emergency Fund?</u>

Your emergency fund should be:

✓ Liquid & Accessible – Savings or high-yield bank accounts.

✓ Low-Risk – Avoid volatile investments (stocks, crypto, real estate).

✓ Separate from Regular Savings – Prevents accidental spending.

? Best Options for Emergency Funds:

? High-Yield Savings Account – Quick access with some interest.

? Fixed Deposits (FDs) with Liquidity Options – Safe and stable.

? Money Market Funds – Low-risk investment with higher returns than savings accounts.

Strategies to Build an Emergency Fund

1?? Automate Monthly Transfers – Set up a recurring transfer to a dedicated emergency account.

2?? Redirect Windfalls – Use bonuses, tax refunds, and side income to boost savings.

3?? Reduce Unnecessary Expenses – Cut down on discretionary spending (subscriptions, dining out).

4?? Start Small, Stay Consistent – Even saving 5–10% of your income regularly makes a difference.

2. Insurance: Mitigating Financial Risks

<u>The Role of Insurance in Financial Resilience</u>

Many people overlook insurance as an essential tool in financial planning. Proper coverage protects your wealth, reduces financial stress, and prevents long-term setbacks.

Types of Essential Insurance

? Health Insurance – Covers medical expenses and hospitalization.

? Life Insurance – Provides financial security to dependents in case of your untimely demise.

? Disability Insurance – Replaces lost income if you are unable to work due to injury or illness.

? Home & Property Insurance – Protects against fire, theft, and natural disasters.

? Liability Insurance – Covers legal expenses if you're sued for damages.

<u>How to Choose the Right Insurance Plans</u>

✔ Compare Plans & Premiums – Look at different insurers and compare benefits vs. costs.

✔ Read the Fine Print – Check coverage limits, exclusions, and hidden clauses.

✔ Assess Your Needs – Consider your lifestyle, dependents, and financial obligations.

✔ Avoid Over-Insurance – Don't pay for unnecessary coverage.

? Pro Tip: Buy health and life insurance early to lock in lower premiums and better coverage.

3. Diversification & Wealth Protection

<u>The Importance of Diversification in Financial Stability</u>

Diversification reduces financial risk by spreading investments across different asset classes, industries, and geographies.

Example of a Diversified Portfolio:

? Equities (Stocks & Mutual Funds) – Growth potential but high risk.

? Real Estate – Stable long-term investment, generates rental income.

? Fixed Deposits & Bonds – Secure, low-risk investments.

? Gold & Precious Metals – Hedge against inflation.

? Cryptocurrency & Alternative Investments – High risk, but potential for high returns.

? <u>How to Diversify Smartly:</u>

✔ Follow the 50/30/20 Rule – 50% in stable investments, 30% in growth assets, 20% in liquid savings.

✔ Rebalance Regularly – Adjust investments based on market conditions and life changes.

✔ Avoid Over-Diversification – Too many small investments can dilute returns.

4. Long-Term Financial Planning & Stability

<u>Retirement Planning & Passive Income</u>

Many people underestimate the cost of retirement and fail to save early enough. Building passive income streams ensures financial stability even when you're not actively earning.

How to Start Retirement Planning

? Start Early – The sooner you invest, the more you benefit from compound interest.

? Use Retirement Accounts – Contribute to tax-advantaged retirement plans (e.g., 401(k), IRA, PPF, NPS).

? Increase Contributions Over Time – Raise your savings rate as income grows.

? Invest in Income-Generating Assets – Real estate, dividend stocks, REITs, and annuities.

<u>The Power of Compound Interest</u>

Example: If you invest $500 per month at an 8% annual return, your savings can grow to:

$150,000 in 15 years.

$500,000 in 30 years.

? Lesson: Small, consistent investments yield massive long-term wealth.

5. Sustainable Financial Habits for Resilience

<u>Mindset Shift for Financial Stability</u>

Financial resilience is more than just earning and saving—it requires a strong mindset and disciplined habits.

Key Financial Habits for Stability

✓ Live Below Your Means – Spend less than you earn.

✓ Track & Optimize Expenses – Use budgeting apps to manage finances.

✓ Eliminate Unnecessary Debt – Pay off high-interest loans first.

✓ Avoid Lifestyle Inflation – Don't increase spending just because income grows.

✓ Invest in Financial Education – Learn about investments, taxes, and personal finance.

Financial Resilience in a Changing Economy

The economy is unpredictable—jobs are lost, businesses fail, and inflation affects purchasing power. To stay financially resilient, you must:

✓ Adapt to Market Changes – Adjust investments based on trends.

✓ Have Multiple Income Streams – Side hustles, freelancing, passive income.

✓ Invest in Skills & Career Growth – Continuous learning ensures employability.

✓ Stay Debt-Free as Much as Possible – Minimize liabilities.

Conclusion

Building financial resilience is not about being rich; it's about being financially secure regardless of economic conditions. By strengthening your financial foundation, preparing for uncertainties, and developing smart habits, you create a safety net that protects and grows your wealth.

? Key Takeaways:

Emergency funds provide financial security during crises.

Insurance protects your assets and loved ones.

Diversification reduces financial risk and ensures stability.

Retirement planning & passive income sustain long-term financial security.

Financial discipline & adaptability are crucial for long-term success.

? Action Plan:

? Start an emergency fund today.

? Review and update your insurance coverage.

? Diversify your investments wisely.

? Build passive income streams for financial freedom.

Financial resilience is a lifelong journey, and by taking proactive steps today, you can ensure a stable, stress-free financial future. ?

CHAPTER THIRTY-FOUR

CREATING LONG-TERM WEALTH & STABILITY

Introduction

Financial stability is not just about earning money—it's about managing, investing, and growing it wisely to ensure long-term wealth. While short-term financial health focuses on budgeting, saving, and avoiding debt, long-term wealth creation involves strategic investments, retirement planning, and financial discipline.

This section will cover retirement planning, wealth-building strategies, tax efficiency, and estate planning, ensuring that you build sustainable financial security for yourself and future generations.

1. Retirement Planning & Passive Income

<u>Why Retirement Planning is Essential</u>

Many people underestimate the importance of early retirement planning. A comfortable retirement is not just about having a pension or savings—it's about having enough passive income to sustain your lifestyle.

? Key Benefits of Early Retirement Planning:

✓ Avoid financial stress in old age.

✓ Take advantage of compound interest for higher returns.

✓ Reduce dependence on children or government pensions.

<u>How Much Do You Need for Retirement?</u>

The 4% Rule is a common benchmark for retirement savings. It suggests that you can safely withdraw 4% of your total savings per year without running out of money.

Formula:

? Required Retirement Corpus = Annual Expenses × 25

Example:

If you need $40,000 per year to maintain your lifestyle:

? $40,000 × 25 = $1,000,000 needed in total savings.

<u>Types of Retirement Accounts & Plans</u>

✓ 401(k) / NPS (National Pension Scheme) / EPF – Employer-sponsored retirement funds.

✓ IRAs (Roth & Traditional) / PPF (Public Provident Fund) – Tax-advantaged retirement savings.

✓ Annuities & Pension Plans – Provide a steady income after retirement.

<u>How to Build Passive Income for Retirement</u>

✓ Dividend Stocks – Invest in companies that pay regular dividends.

✓ Rental Properties – Earn consistent rental income.

✓ Mutual Funds & Index Funds – Grow wealth with minimal effort.

✓ REITs (Real Estate Investment Trusts) – Real estate income without managing properties.

✓ Bonds & Fixed Deposits – Secure, low-risk income streams.

? Pro Tip: Automate retirement contributions to ensure consistent savings.

2. Wealth-Building Strategies

<u>The Power of Investing</u>

Investing is the key to growing wealth over time. Savings alone will not create wealth because inflation erodes purchasing power.

How to Start Investing for Wealth Creation

1?? Set Clear Financial Goals – Short-term (1–5 years), medium-term (5–10 years), and long-term (10+ years).

2?? Choose the Right Asset Classes – Balance between stocks, real estate, bonds, and alternative investments.

3?? Diversify Your Portfolio – Avoid putting all money in one asset.

4?? Stay Consistent & Invest Regularly – Dollar-cost averaging reduces market risk.

5?? Monitor & Rebalance Portfolio Annually – Adjust investments based on market changes.

Best Investment Options for Long-Term Wealth

? Stock Market – Historically provides 8-12% annual returns over long periods.

? Real Estate – Appreciates in value while generating rental income.

? Gold & Commodities – Hedge against inflation and economic downturns.

? Business & Entrepreneurship – Building a business can generate massive wealth.

How to Minimize Investment Risks

✓ Research before investing.

✓ Avoid speculative and high-risk investments without due diligence.

✓ Stick to long-term wealth-building strategies, not quick gains.

? Pro Tip: Avoid emotional investing—fear and greed can lead to poor decisions.

3. Tax Planning & Wealth Preservation

<u>Why Tax Planning is Crucial for Wealth Building</u>

Proper tax planning can save you thousands of dollars over your lifetime. High taxes reduce investment returns, slowing down wealth accumulation.

Tax-Efficient Investment Strategies

✓ Use Tax-Advantaged Accounts – 401(k), IRA, PPF, NPS, and Roth IRAs grow tax-free.[Ch VIA Onwards for India]

✓ Invest in Tax-Efficient Funds – ETFs and index funds have lower tax burdens.

✓ Capitalize on Tax Deductions – Home loans, education, and medical expenses offer tax benefits.

✓ Harvest Tax Losses – Offset capital gains by selling underperforming assets.

Common Tax-Saving Strategies

? Retirement Contributions – Max out tax-deferred retirement accounts.

? Capital Gains Management – Hold investments longer to qualify for lower long-term capital gains tax.

? Trusts & Estate Planning – Reduce inheritance tax and protect wealth for heirs.

? Pro Tip: Consult a tax advisor to legally minimize tax liabilities.

4. Estate Planning: Securing Wealth for Future Generations

<u>Why Estate Planning is Important</u>

Many people neglect estate planning, but without a clear plan, wealth can be lost due to taxes, legal disputes, or mismanagement.

Key Goals of Estate Planning:

✓ Ensure your wealth is transferred according to your wishes.

✓ Minimize inheritance tax and legal complications.

✓ Protect assets for future generations.

Essential Estate Planning Tools

? Will – A legally binding document specifying how assets should be distributed.

? Trusts – Helps manage and protect wealth for heirs while reducing estate taxes.

? Power of Attorney – Appoints someone to handle financial matters if incapacitated.

? Beneficiary Designations – Ensures assets (insurance, retirement accounts) go directly to intended heirs.

? Pro Tip: Review your estate plan every 5 years or after major life events (marriage, children, divorce).

5. Sustaining Wealth for Generations

<u>Avoiding Lifestyle Inflation</u>

One of the biggest threats to long-term wealth is lifestyle inflation—as income grows, spending increases proportionally, preventing wealth accumulation.

✓ Live Below Your Means – Don't upgrade your lifestyle every time income increases.

✓ Invest Instead of Spending Extra Income – Prioritize long-term wealth over short-term luxuries.

✓ Avoid Debt-Fueled Consumption – Don't take loans for non-essential expenses.

Financial Education for Future Generations

To ensure long-term family wealth, it's essential to educate your children and heirs on financial management.

? How to Teach Financial Responsibility:

✓ Involve family in financial discussions.

✓ Teach children about budgeting, saving, and investing early.

✓ Encourage responsible spending and wealth-building habits.

Giving Back & Philanthropy

For many wealthy individuals, legacy isn't just about money—it's about impact.

✓ Create a Family Foundation – Support charitable causes you care about.

✓ Set Up a Charitable Trust – Donate wealth efficiently while receiving tax benefits.

✓ Encourage Responsible Giving – Teach future generations about philanthropy.

? Pro Tip: Wealth is meaningful when it improves lives beyond your own.

Conclusion

Creating long-term wealth and stability requires planning, discipline, and smart financial decisions. The goal is not just to accumulate money but to create lasting financial security for yourself and future generations.

Key Takeaways:

Retirement planning ensures financial independence in later years.

Investing wisely builds sustainable wealth.

Tax planning minimizes unnecessary losses.

Estate planning secures wealth for the next generation.

Financial discipline prevents lifestyle inflation and reckless spending.

? Action Plan:

? Start investing in long-term assets today.

? Maximize tax-advantaged retirement contributions.

? Draft a will and create an estate plan.

? Teach financial responsibility to the next generation.

By following these principles, you can build a secure financial future that lasts for generations. ?

CHAPTER THIRTY-FIVE

FINANCIAL INDEPENDENCE & THE FUTURE OF MONEY

Introduction

Financial independence is the ability to sustain your lifestyle without actively working for money. It means having enough passive income, savings, and investments to cover your expenses indefinitely. Achieving financial independence allows you to pursue your passions, retire early, and enjoy life without financial stress.

As the world evolves, so does the financial landscape. Technology, digital currencies, automation, and economic shifts are changing how we earn, save, and invest money. This section explores how to achieve financial independence and prepare for the future of money.

1. Defining Financial Independence

What is Financial Independence?

Financial independence is achieved when your passive income exceeds your monthly expenses, allowing you to live comfortably without relying on a job.

Key Indicators of Financial Independence:

✓ Passive income covers 100% of essential expenses.

✓ No high-interest debt.

✓ Substantial retirement savings.

✔ Ability to work by choice, not necessity.

The FIRE Movement (Financial Independence, Retire Early)

FIRE is a growing movement where individuals aim to save aggressively and invest early to achieve financial freedom decades before the traditional retirement age.

? Types of FIRE Strategies:

Lean FIRE – Living frugally and saving aggressively.

Fat FIRE – Achieving financial freedom while maintaining a high-spending lifestyle.

Coast FIRE – Investing early and letting compound interest do the work.

Barista FIRE – Achieving financial freedom but continuing to work part-time.

? How to Calculate Your FIRE Number:

? FIRE Number = Annual Expenses × 25

(Example: If you need $40,000 per year, you need $1,000,000 in investments.)

2. Steps to Achieve Financial Independence

1?? Increase Savings Rate

✔ Aim to save 50% or more of your income.

✔ Cut unnecessary expenses and avoid lifestyle inflation.

✔ Automate savings to remove temptation.

2?? Create Multiple Income Streams

Relying on a single paycheck is risky. Diversify your income sources:

? Passive Income – Stocks, dividends, rental properties.

? Side Hustles – Freelancing, consulting, online businesses.

? Digital Assets – YouTube, e-books, online courses.

3?? Invest Aggressively & Wisely

Your money should work for you, not sit idle in a savings account.

? Best Investment Strategies for Financial Independence:

✔ Index Funds & ETFs – Low-risk, long term stock market growth.

✔ Real Estate – Passive rental income and capital appreciation.

✔ Dividend Stocks – Steady income from company profits.

✔ Cryptocurrency & Blockchain Investments – High risk but potential for massive returns.

4?? Eliminate Debt Quickly

Debt slows down financial freedom. Focus on paying off high-interest debt first.

? Debt Payoff Strategies:

✔ Avalanche Method – Pay off highest interest first.

✔ Snowball Method – Pay off smallest debt first for motivation.

✔ Refinancing Loans – Lower interest rates to reduce financial burden.
5?? Reduce Expenses Without Sacrificing Quality of Life
Frugality is not deprivation—it's prioritization.

? Practical Cost-Cutting Strategies:

✔ Cut subscription services you don't use.

✔ Cook meals at home instead of eating out.

✔ Buy second-hand or refurbished electronics.

✔ Travel smart with discounts and off-season deals.

? Key Rule: Every dollar saved is another dollar invested towards financial independence.

3. The Future of Money: Technology & Digital Finance

1?? The Rise of Fintech & Digital Banking

Technology is transforming financial services. Traditional banking is being replaced by fintech apps, AI-driven investments, and decentralized finance (DeFi).

✔ Robo-Advisors – AI-powered investment platforms (Wealthfront, Betterment).

✔ Digital-Only Banks – Online banking with no physical branches (Revolut, Chime).

✔ Blockchain & Smart Contracts – Automating transactions without middlemen.

2?? Cryptocurrency & Decentralized Finance (DeFi)

Cryptocurrency is reshaping how people save, invest, and transfer money.

? Key Cryptocurrencies to Watch:

✔ Bitcoin (BTC) – The most well-known digital store of value.

✔ Ethereum (ETH) – Supports smart contracts and decentralized apps.

✔ Stablecoins (USDT, USDC) – Digital assets pegged to fiat currency.

? DeFi Trends to Watch:

✔ Decentralized Exchanges (DEXs) – Peer-to-peer trading without banks.

✔ Yield Farming & Staking – Earning interest by holding digital assets.

✔ NFTs & Tokenization – Digital ownership of assets.

? Caution: While crypto offers high potential returns, it is highly volatile and should be only a small percentage (5-10%) of your portfolio.

4. How AI & Automation Are Changing Personal Finance

1?? AI-Driven Investing & Financial Planning

✔ Robo-advisors analyze risk and recommend investments.

✔ AI-powered budgeting apps track spending habits.

✔ Automated tax optimization tools help reduce tax liabilities.

2?? The Role of Automation in Wealth Building

✔ Automated Savings Plans – Transfers money into savings without manual effort.

✔ Recurring Investments – Dollar-cost averaging in stocks, ETFs, or crypto.

✔ Smart Bill Pay – Avoids late fees and maintains credit score.

? Takeaway: Embracing financial automation helps eliminate human error, emotional spending, and missed opportunities.

5. Sustaining Financial Independence for a Lifetime

1?? Avoiding Wealth Erosion

Many people achieve financial independence but lose wealth due to poor financial management.

? How to Protect Your Wealth:

✔ Avoid Get-Rich-Quick Schemes – If it sounds too good to be true, it is.

✔ Stay Educated – Keep up with market trends and financial news.

✔ Maintain a Long-Term Mindset – Avoid panic selling during market downturns.

2?? Teaching Financial Literacy to Future Generations

Financial independence should be passed down. Teaching children how to manage money wisely ensures generational wealth.

✔ Teach budgeting, investing, and the importance of savings.

✔ Set up education funds, trusts, and inheritance planning.

✔ Encourage financial independence instead of entitlement.

3?? Embracing Minimalism & Value-Based Living

Financial independence isn't just about having more money—it's about needing less.

✔ Focus on experiences over material possessions.

✔ Prioritize health, relationships, and personal growth.

✔ Design a lifestyle that brings happiness without financial stress.

? Final Thought: True wealth is not just financial—it's about freedom, security, and peace of mind.

Conclusion

Financial independence is achievable for anyone willing to make disciplined choices. The key is to earn, save, invest, and adapt to financial trends.

Key Takeaways:

✓ Save aggressively and invest early for long-term wealth.

✓ Create multiple income streams to reduce reliance on one source.

✓ Eliminate debt to avoid financial burdens.

✓ Embrace digital finance and stay ahead of financial innovations.

✓ Automate and optimize finances for stress-free money management.

✓ Pass down financial literacy to future generations for lasting wealth.

? Final Action Plan:

? Set a FIRE goal and calculate your financial independence number.

? Invest in assets that generate passive income.

? Use automation to simplify your finances.

? Stay informed about future financial trends.

By mastering financial independence and the future of money, you position yourself for a life of freedom, security, and limitless opportunities. ?

Freedom & Decision-Making: Are You Really in Control?

CHAPTER THIRTY-SIX

Understanding Freedom and Control

1.1 The Illusion of Free Will

One of the most debated topics in philosophy, psychology, and neuroscience is the question of free will—do we truly have control over our choices, or is our freedom an illusion?

At first glance, it seems obvious that we make our own decisions. We decide what to eat, where to work, whom to marry, and how to spend our time. But if we dig deeper, the very nature of choice becomes questionable.

<u>The Philosophical Dilemma: Free Will vs. Determinism</u>

Philosophers have long argued whether humans possess genuine autonomy or if all decisions are merely pre-determined by past events, biological makeup, and environmental conditions.

Determinism states that all events, including human actions, are predetermined by existing conditions and past events. If everything follows a cause-and-effect pattern, then the idea of freely choosing is merely an illusion.

Libertarianism argues that free will is real and that we, as conscious agents, make independent choices that are not determined by prior causes.

Compatibilism tries to merge the two, suggesting that while our choices are influenced by external factors, we still have a subjective sense of control that gives meaning to decision-making.

If determinism holds true, does this mean we are merely puppets of nature and nurture? If libertarianism is correct, how do we explain scientific studies that suggest our decisions may be made subconsciously before we even realize them?

<u>Psychological Studies on Free Will</u>

Neurological experiments reveal that the brain often makes decisions before we are consciously aware of them.

A famous experiment by Benjamin Libet (1983) showed that electrical activity in the brain's motor cortex occurs milliseconds before a person consciously "decides" to act. This suggests that our conscious mind is not the initiator but rather the observer of decisions already made at a subconscious level.

More recent research using functional MRI scans shows that brain activity can predict a person's decision up to 10 seconds before they consciously decide.

If our brain decides before we do, where is the freedom in our choices?

1.2 The Social Conditioning of Freedom

Even if we assume some level of free will, how much of it is truly ours? From the moment we are born, we are shaped by our culture, society, education, and upbringing. These factors predefine our preferences, beliefs, and even what we consider "acceptable" choices.

<u>How Society Shapes Our Choices</u>

Consider the following examples:

Career Paths: Are you truly choosing your career, or were your interests shaped by societal norms, family pressure, or financial necessity?

Relationships: Many people feel compelled to marry, have children, or conform to gender roles simply because of societal expectations, not because of personal desire.

Success & Wealth: The definition of "success" is largely determined by external conditioning—higher income, luxury possessions, and social status. Is this what you really want, or have you been trained to desire it?

We often believe we are making independent choices, but those choices are heavily conditioned.

<u>The Role of Media and Marketing in Decision-Making</u>

Marketing, advertising, and social media play a powerful role in shaping our desires and beliefs.

Advertisements exploit psychological triggers (scarcity, social proof, authority bias) to push people into "choosing" products they otherwise wouldn't have considered.

Social media algorithms feed people personalized content, reinforcing their existing beliefs rather than allowing them to think independently.

Many people imitate celebrities and influencers, subconsciously following trends rather than making truly individual choices.

If our choices are manipulated by external forces, can we still claim to be free thinkers?

1.3 Biological and Neurological Limitations

Beyond societal conditioning, our decisions are also constrained by biological and neurological factors.

<u>The Brain's Decision-Making Process</u>

The prefrontal cortex is responsible for rational thinking and long-term planning, while the limbic system (including the amygdala) drives emotional and instinctive responses. Many decisions are a tug-of-war between these two systems.

For example:

When choosing between eating healthy or indulging in junk food, the prefrontal cortex (logic) suggests the healthy option, but the limbic system (desire) craves immediate pleasure.

When making financial decisions, the fear center (amygdala) can cause hesitation, even when logic suggests taking calculated risks.

Thus, even within our own minds, we are not fully in control—different brain regions battle for dominance in our choices.

<u>The Role of Genetics in Choices</u>

Studies suggest that genetic factors influence personality traits, including impulsivity, risk-taking behavior, and emotional stability—all of which shape decision-making.

Twin studies show that identical twins raised in different environments often display similar decision-making patterns, proving that biology plays a significant role.

While we might believe we act purely out of logic, our DNA often predetermines our tendencies.

How Hormones and Neurotransmitters Influence Decisions

Dopamine (the pleasure chemical) influences addiction, motivation, and reward-seeking behavior.

Cortisol (the stress hormone) causes fear-based decisions, often leading to playing it safe instead of taking bold actions.

Serotonin levels impact mood and confidence, influencing how people approach choices in daily life.

Our neurochemical balance shifts daily based on sleep, diet, stress, and emotions—meaning that even the same person may make different decisions depending on biological fluctuations.

Conclusion: Are We Really in Control?

After examining philosophy, psychology, society, and biology, one thing becomes clear: absolute freedom in decision-making is a myth.

However, this does not mean that we are completely powerless. While many of our choices are influenced, we can take steps to increase our awareness and regain some control:

Ways to Take Back Control of Your Decisions

Develop Self-Awareness: Recognize how society, biology, and emotions influence your choices.

Practice Mindful Decision-Making: Slow down and evaluate decisions instead of acting on impulse.

Reduce External Manipulation: Limit exposure to marketing, social media, and societal expectations.

Strengthen Rational Thinking: Train your prefrontal cortex through journaling, logical reasoning, and decision-making frameworks.

Accept and Adapt: While we may not have complete control, recognizing our influences allows us to make better, more conscious choices.

Thus, true freedom lies not in having absolute control but in understanding the forces shaping our decisions and learning to navigate them wisely.

CHAPTER THIRTY-SEVEN

The Psychology of Decision-Making

2.1 The Conscious vs. Subconscious Mind

Many of us believe that we make conscious decisions—that we rationally weigh options and pick the best choice. However, research shows that most decisions occur subconsciously before we are even aware of them.

<u>The Power of the Subconscious Mind</u>

Studies estimate that 95% of daily decisions are made subconsciously, while only 5% involve active, rational thinking.

The subconscious mind processes millions of bits of information per second, compared to the conscious mind, which can handle only about 40 bits per second.

Our past experiences, emotions, and habits store themselves in the subconscious, influencing our automatic reactions and preferences.

<u>Cognitive Biases and Heuristics</u>

Our brains rely on mental shortcuts (heuristics) to make decisions faster, but these often lead to irrational biases:

Confirmation Bias: We seek out information that confirms what we already believe, ignoring contradictory evidence.

Anchoring Bias: Our decisions are influenced by the first piece of information we receive (e.g., pricing strategies in marketing).

Availability Heuristic: We judge the probability of events based on how easily they come to mind (e.g., fearing plane crashes more than car accidents).

Loss Aversion: We fear losing more than we enjoy gaining, leading to risk-averse behavior.

These biases explain why people often make irrational financial, personal, and career choices, thinking they are being rational when in reality, they are being subconsciously influenced.

<u>Experiments on Subconscious Decision-Making</u>

Benjamin Libet's Experiment (1983): Showed that brain activity occurs milliseconds before people consciously "decide" to move a finger, suggesting that our subconscious mind makes decisions before our awareness catches up.

John-Dylan Haynes' Research (2008): Using brain scans, he found that a person's choice between two buttons could be predicted up to 10 seconds before they consciously decided.

This research raises a crucial question: If our subconscious determines choices before we are aware, how much control do we really have?

2.2 The Role of Emotions in Decision-Making

<u>The Myth of Rationality</u>

Most people believe they make logical decisions, but in reality, emotions play a dominant role. Neuroscientist Antonio Damasio discovered that people who suffered brain damage in areas that process emotions struggled to make decisions—even simple ones like choosing a meal. This proves that emotions are not just a distraction but are central to decision-making.

Fear-Based vs. Desire-Based Decisions

<u>Fear-Based Decisions (Avoidance)</u>

Rooted in anxiety, uncertainty, or past trauma.

Examples:

Staying in a toxic job due to fear of financial insecurity.

Avoiding investments because of past financial losses.

Not expressing feelings due to fear of rejection.

<u>Desire-Based Decisions (Impulse & Pleasure-Seeking)</u>

Driven by dopamine and reward systems.

Examples:

Buying an expensive gadget impulsively.

Choosing an unhealthy meal over a nutritious one.

Chasing short-term pleasure over long-term goals.

While fear keeps us safe, excessive fear can lead to paralysis. Likewise, chasing desires without discipline leads to impulse-driven mistakes.

<u>Regret and Decision Paralysis</u>

"What if I had chosen differently?"—Regret often distorts our perception of past decisions.

Choice Overload: Too many options can cause decision fatigue, making people more likely to avoid making a choice altogether.

The "Sunk Cost Fallacy": People stick with bad choices because they already invested time/money, even when leaving would be wiser.

Understanding emotions helps in making better, balanced choices, instead of reacting impulsively or out of fear.

2.3 External Influences: Are We Being Manipulated?

Our decisions are not made in a vacuum. Every day, external forces manipulate our thinking—often without us realizing it.

<u>Social Proof and Peer Pressure</u>

Humans are wired to follow the majority due to evolutionary survival instincts.

The Asch Conformity Experiments (1951) showed that people would give the wrong answer to a simple question just because others did.

Examples in daily life:

Buying a product because it has thousands of 5-star reviews.

Following a trend just because "everyone is doing it".

Choosing a career or partner based on society's expectations.

The Influence of Authority in decision making:People tend to obey authority figures even when they believe an action is wrong (Milgram's Obedience Study proved this with shocking results).

Doctors and experts influence medical choices.

Teachers and parents shape career decisions.

Political leaders and laws dictate what is "acceptable" behavior.

<u>The Role of Advertising and Psychological Manipulation</u>

Companies study human psychology to make people buy things they don't need.

Techniques used:

Scarcity ("Only 2 left in stock!")

Urgency ("Sale ends in 24 hours!")

Emotional Appeal (Fear, happiness, nostalgia in ads): Most people believe they are immune to marketing, yet every purchase, belief, and habit is shaped by carefully crafted psychological strategies.

Social Media & Algorithmic Influence :Platforms like Facebook, Instagram, and TikTok use AI to feed users content that aligns with their biases, reinforcing their worldview instead of challenging it.

Echo chambers trap people in limited perspectives, making independent decision-making harder.

Dopamine loops (likes, comments, notifications) keep people addicted, reducing critical thinking skills.

The more we understand these influences, the better we can resist being unconsciously controlled.

Conclusion: Can We Regain Control Over Our Decisions?

The psychology of decision-making reveals that:

Most decisions are subconscious before we are aware of them.

Emotions drive choices more than logic.

External forces (social, authority, advertising, technology) manipulate our decisions.

How to Take Back Control

Train Yourself to Identify Biases

Ask: Am I making this choice logically, or is a bias/emotion influencing me?

Keep a decision journal to track patterns in thinking.

Use Decision-Making Frameworks

The 10/10/10 Rule (How will I feel about this choice in 10 minutes, 10 months, 10 years?)

First Principles Thinking (Break down a decision into its fundamental truths).

Delay Emotional Decisions

If feeling impulsive, wait 24 hours before deciding.

If feeling afraid, ask if the fear is real or conditioned.

Limit External Influences

Reduce social media and advertising exposure.

Make decisions based on personal values, not societal expectations.

Practice Self-Reflection

Meditation, journaling, or deep thinking exercises can help reconnect with inner wisdom instead of external noise.

Final Thought

You may never have absolute control over your decisions, but by understanding how your mind works, you can make more intentional, conscious choices.

True freedom is not about having unlimited choices; it is about understanding the forces shaping them and learning to navigate them wisely.

CHAPTER THIRTY-EIGHT

CONSTRAINTS ON FREEDOM: WHAT HOLDS YOU BACK?

Freedom is often viewed as the ability to make independent choices, yet most people feel trapped by circumstances beyond their control. While we may think we are free to decide, various internal and external constraints limit our autonomy. These constraints can be financial, psychological, societal, or technological, making it crucial to recognize what truly holds us back from making independent decisions.

3.1 Economic and Financial Dependencies

<u>Money as a Limiter of Freedom</u>

In modern society, financial stability dictates personal freedom. Many of our decisions are shaped by economic conditions, and often, we feel like prisoners of our financial situation.

Examples of Financial Dependency

Career Choices: Many people stay in jobs they dislike because they need financial security. Even when an opportunity for a more fulfilling career arises, the fear of losing a paycheck holds them back.

Debt and Loans: Credit card debt, student loans, and mortgages act as modern chains, limiting one's ability to take risks.

Golden Handcuffs: High salaries and corporate benefits create a paradox: while people earn more, they feel trapped because leaving means losing financial stability.

Consumerism: Are You Really Choosing What to Buy?

Society conditions us to desire luxury brands and material possessions, often spending money on things we don't need.

The pressure to maintain a certain lifestyle standard (big house, expensive car, lavish vacations) forces people to make financially unsound decisions.

Even when people achieve financial freedom, social comparison pushes them to spend more rather than use their resources for true independence.

<u>Breaking Free from Financial Constraints</u>

Minimalism & Smart Spending: Prioritize needs over wants to avoid being a slave to money.

Financial Independence: Develop multiple income sources to reduce reliance on a single employer.

Investing in Freedom: Save money not just for survival but for buying back time and choice.

If financial dependency controls your decisions, how free are you really?

3.2 The Fear Factor: Why We Avoid True Freedom

<u>Fear of Uncertainty: The Root of Inaction</u>

Most people do not actively seek freedom because uncertainty is terrifying. When presented with an opportunity to break free from constraints, the human brain defaults to safety.

Why Do People Fear Change?

The Comfort Zone Illusion: The mind perceives familiarity as safety, even when it is unfulfilling.

Loss Aversion: The fear of losing something (money, status, relationships) outweighs the potential benefits of change.

Negative Conditioning: Since childhood, we are taught to avoid risks ("Play it safe," "Get a stable job"), discouraging us from making bold moves.

<u>Fear-Based Decision Making: How It Limits You</u>

Fear of Failure: Many people never start businesses, change careers, or take risks because they are afraid of failing.

Fear of Judgment: The opinions of others dictate our choices—people avoid unconventional paths because they fear criticism.

Fear of Regret: Some remain in bad relationships or careers because they fear regretting the decision later.

<u>How to Overcome Fear and Take Back Control</u>

Shift Focus from Fear to Growth: Instead of asking, "What if I fail?" ask, "What if I succeed?"

Desensitization to Uncertainty: Make small, calculated risks regularly to get comfortable with change.

Challenge Negative Conditioning: Identify where your fears come from (society, family, past experiences) and actively reframe them.

Freedom is often avoided not because it is impossible but because it is uncomfortable.

3.3 Technology and the Modern Age of Control

While technology has increased access to information and opportunities, it has also introduced a new layer of control over our decision-making process. From algorithmic manipulation to digital addiction, modern technology subtly influences our choices more than we realize.

<u>Social Media and the Illusion of Choice</u>

Platforms like Facebook, Instagram, and Twitter present themselves as tools for free expression, yet they shape and restrict the way we think.

Algorithmic Influence: AI curates what we see, reinforcing our existing beliefs rather than exposing us to diverse perspectives.

Echo Chambers & Filter Bubbles: We are trapped in personalized digital realities, making it difficult to form independent opinions.

Social Validation Loop: Likes, comments, and shares trigger dopamine responses, making people crave approval rather than authentic self-expression.

<u>Surveillance and Data Control</u>

Governments, corporations, and advertisers collect vast amounts of data on individuals, creating psychological profiles to predict and influence behavior.

Privacy is a Myth: Every click, search, and conversation is tracked to shape future decisions.

Behavioral Prediction & Manipulation: Ads and content are tailored to your habits, insecurities, and preferences to make you act in specific ways.

AI and Decision-Making: Artificial intelligence systems increasingly make choices for us (Netflix suggestions, Google search results), limiting independent thinking.

<u>Breaking Free from Technological Control</u>

Digital Detox & Conscious Usage: Limit time spent on algorithm-driven platforms.

Diversify Information Sources: Actively seek opposing viewpoints to counteract filter bubbles.

Strengthen Privacy Awareness: Use encrypted apps, limit data-sharing, and question online content.

The more dependent we become on external digital systems, the less control we have over our own decisions.

3.4 Social and Cultural Constraints

How much of your personality, values, and decisions are truly your own, and how much is programmed by society?

<u>Cultural Expectations as Invisible Chains</u>

Career Pressure: Societies often dictate which careers are "respectable" (doctor, engineer, lawyer) while discouraging unconventional paths.

Gender Roles: Traditional expectations limit personal freedom (e.g., women expected to prioritize family over careers, men expected to suppress emotions).

Marriage & Family Expectations: Social pressure to marry, have children, and follow conventional life paths restricts personal choice.

<u>Religious and Moral Conditioning</u>

Many beliefs about right and wrong are inherited, not independently formed.

Fear of Rejection: People often conform to religious and societal norms to fit in, even when they disagree internally.

Breaking the Mold is Punished: Those who challenge societal norms often face criticism, exclusion, or isolation.

<u>How to Free Yourself from Social Conditioning</u>

Question Your Beliefs: Identify what values you truly believe in versus what you were taught to believe.

Expose Yourself to Different Cultures: Travel, read, and meet people with different backgrounds to challenge ingrained assumptions.

Stop Seeking Approval: Make choices based on personal fulfillment, not societal validation.

If society controls what you believe is possible, then how much of your life is really yours?

Conclusion: Understanding and Overcoming Constraints

While we may never achieve absolute freedom, recognizing these constraints gives us power over them.

<u>Key Takeaways</u>

Financial Dependency forces people to make survival-driven rather than passion-driven choices.

Fear of uncertainty keeps people stuck in unfulfilling situations.

Technology manipulates thought patterns, limiting true autonomy.

Social & cultural conditioning programs people to conform rather than create their own paths.

<u>Steps to Reclaim Your Freedom</u>

Build Financial Security: Work towards financial independence so money doesn't control your choices.

Challenge Fear Regularly: Small risks develop the courage to make bigger life changes.

Reduce Digital Dependence: Take control of your screen time and information sources.

Redefine Success on Your Terms: Live based on personal values rather than societal expectations.

Freedom is not just about having choices—it is about understanding what limits your choices and actively working to remove those constraints.

CHAPTER THIRTY-NINE

BREAKING FREE – HOW TO TAKE CONTROL OF YOUR DECISIONS

In previous sections, we explored how external and internal constraints limit our decision-making. From societal pressures and financial dependencies to technological manipulation and subconscious biases, our choices are rarely as free as we think. However, while absolute freedom may not be possible, reclaiming control over our decisions is.

This section provides practical strategies to break free from these constraints and regain autonomy in decision-making. By cultivating self-awareness, developing deliberate decision-making habits, and redefining success on our own terms, we can move closer to genuine independence.

4.1 Building Self-Awareness: The Foundation of True Freedom

Before we can change our decision-making patterns, we must first understand why we make the choices we do.

<u>The Power of Self-Awareness in Decision-Making</u>

Self-awareness allows us to:

Identify external influences shaping our choices.

Recognize cognitive biases affecting judgment.

Understand emotional triggers that lead to impulsive or fear-based decisions.

Define personal values that align with meaningful choices.

Without self-awareness, we remain puppets of our subconscious and external forces.

Practical Steps to Develop Self-Awareness

Journaling for Reflection
Write down major decisions you've made in the past year.
Ask: Was this decision truly mine, or was it influenced by others (family, society, media)?
Identify patterns in your choices and whether they align with your core values.
Mindfulness & Meditation
Mindfulness helps you observe thoughts and emotions without acting on them impulsively.
Daily meditation (even 5-10 minutes) can improve focus, emotional control, and clarity in decision-making.
Personality & Bias Assessments
Take tests like MBTI, Enneagram, or Big Five Personality Traits to understand how you process decisions.
Study common cognitive biases (confirmation bias, loss aversion, authority bias) to recognize when they distort thinking.
By improving self-awareness, you regain control over your thoughts and decisions rather than letting them control you.

4.2 The Art of Deliberate Choice: Making Decisions with Intention
Most people operate on autopilot, reacting to life rather than actively shaping it. To break free, we must develop a habit of deliberate decision-making—choosing consciously, not impulsively.
How to Make Better Decisions
Use the 10/10/10 Rule
When facing a choice, ask:
How will I feel about this in 10 minutes?
How will I feel about this in 10 months?
How will I feel about this in 10 years?
This method helps differentiate short-term emotions from long-term consequences.
First Principles Thinking (Breaking Down Choices)
Instead of making decisions based on societal assumptions, break them down into fundamental truths:
Example: Instead of choosing a career based on prestige, ask: What work truly excites me, regardless of social validation?
Reframe Fear as a Guide
Instead of avoiding fear, use it as an indicator:

If you're afraid of a choice because it challenges comfort zones, it may be the right move for growth.

Differentiate rational fear (danger) from irrational fear (self-doubt, social judgment).

Adopt the "Opportunity Cost" Mindset

Every decision means giving up an alternative. Ask: What is the cost of NOT making this decision?

Helps eliminate paralysis by analysis and overthinking.

By training yourself to think deliberately rather than reactively, you begin making choices aligned with your authentic self rather than external expectations.

4.3 Redefining Success and Autonomy: Living on Your Own Terms

One of the biggest barriers to freedom is societal conditioning on success. Many people make decisions based on external validation (status, wealth, social approval) rather than internal fulfillment.

The Trap of Conventional Success

Society defines success as money, career prestige, social status.

People chase titles, degrees, and material wealth—often at the expense of true happiness.

Many who achieve "success" still feel unfulfilled, realizing they lived by others' definitions instead of their own.

How to Redefine Success for Yourself

Ask: What Does an "Ideal Life" Look Like for Me?

Instead of chasing predefined goals, visualize your ideal life without societal influence.

Example: If you had financial security, what would you truly want to do daily?

Measure Success by Freedom, Not Status

Instead of asking, How much money can I make?, ask, How much freedom does this decision give me?

If a high-paying job limits time, creativity, and fulfillment, is it truly success?

Prioritize Purpose Over Prestige

Success should be measured by impact, fulfillment, and personal values, not just external markers.

When you redefine success on your own terms, your decision-making becomes more authentic and aligned with your personal freedom.

4.4 Reducing External Influence: Taking Back Control

Even with self-awareness, deliberate decision-making, and a new definition of success, external forces will still try to influence you. To truly regain control, you must limit their impact.

<u>How to Resist External Manipulation</u>

Social Media Detox & Mindful Consumption

Limit exposure to algorithm-driven content that shapes beliefs unconsciously.

Curate your feeds to reduce toxic comparison and influence.

Identify & Remove Toxic Influences

Surround yourself with people who encourage independent thinking, not conformity.

Distance yourself from relationships, workplaces, and environments that limit your autonomy.

Develop a "Question Everything" Mindset

Before making a choice, ask:

Am I choosing this because I truly want it or because I'm conditioned to want it?

Who benefits from this decision?

Create "Freedom Habits"

Set personal boundaries to avoid being pressured into decisions.

Practice saying no to obligations that don't align with your values.

The more you reduce external control over your choices, the more you cultivate independent thinking and genuine autonomy.

4.5 Designing a Life of Intentional Freedom

Finally, regaining control is not just about making better decisions today—it's about creating a lifestyle that continuously supports independent thinking and choice.

<u>How to Live with True Autonomy</u>

Time Ownership

The ultimate form of freedom is control over your time.

Design a life where you dictate your schedule, rather than others controlling it.

Financial Independence

Build income sources that give you flexibility and choice.

Avoid financial traps that force dependence on employers, debt, or external conditions.

Minimalism & Essentialism

Reduce unnecessary commitments, distractions, and material dependencies.

Focus on what truly matters rather than accumulating things or obligations.

Self-Directed Learning

Commit to lifelong learning, developing skills that allow self-reliance and adaptability.

By designing life around freedom rather than obligation, you gain true autonomy over your choices and actions.

Conclusion: The Path to True Control

Freedom is not about having endless choices—it is about having the clarity, self-awareness, and courage to make decisions that align with your authentic self.

<u>Summary of Key Steps</u>

Develop Self-Awareness: Understand what drives your decisions.

Practice Deliberate Decision-Making: Move from autopilot to conscious choices.

Redefine Success: Align goals with personal fulfillment, not societal standards.

Limit External Influences: Reduce manipulation from society, media, and culture.

Design an Intentional Life: Prioritize freedom, fulfillment, and purpose.

By applying these strategies, you regain control over your mind, choices, and life, moving toward true personal freedom.

CHAPTER FORTY

PRACTICAL STEPS TO REGAIN CONTROL

In the previous sections, we examined the constraints on freedom, the psychology of decision-making, and how external forces shape our choices. Now, it's time to focus on actionable steps to regain control over your life and decisions. True freedom doesn't mean having no restrictions at all—it means having the clarity, autonomy, and discipline to make decisions that align with your values and long-term goals.

This section provides practical strategies to:

Improve decision-making

Reduce external manipulation

Strengthen independent thinking

Develop habits that support long-term freedom

5.1 Mental Models for Better Decision-Making

<u>Why Mental Models Matter</u>

Mental models are thinking frameworks that help us make rational, informed decisions. Instead of relying on emotions or impulse, these models help us analyze choices logically and effectively.

<u>Key Mental Models to Improve Decisions</u>

First Principles Thinking (Break Down the Problem)

Ask: What are the fundamental truths of this situation?

Instead of following conventional wisdom, rebuild knowledge from scratch.

Example: Instead of assuming a career path is "safe," question if it truly aligns with financial stability and personal fulfillment.

The 80/20 Rule (Focus on High-Impact Actions)

80% of results come from 20% of actions. Identify which actions create the most value and prioritize them.

Example: Instead of working 10-hour days on low-value tasks, focus on the few key tasks that drive real progress.

Opportunity Cost (Consider the Trade-Offs)

Every decision comes at the cost of another opportunity. Ask: What am I giving up by making this choice?

Helps in avoiding distractions and staying aligned with priorities.

The Eisenhower Matrix (Urgency vs. Importance)

Categorize tasks into:

Urgent & Important (Do immediately)

Important but Not Urgent (Schedule time for them)

Urgent but Not Important (Delegate them)

Neither Urgent nor Important (Eliminate them)

Helps in avoiding reactive decision-making and focusing on long-term goals.

The Regret Minimization Framework

Developed by Jeff Bezos, this model asks: At age 80, will I regret not taking this action?

Helps in making bold decisions and overcoming fear of uncertainty.

5.2 Reducing External Influence

<u>Break Free from Social Conditioning</u>

Society dictates how we should think, behave, and define success.

To regain control, question everything you've been told and seek alternative perspectives.

How to Reduce Social Influence

Limit Social Media Consumption

Social media feeds bias, comparison, and emotional manipulation.

Take regular detoxes and curate content consciously.

Challenge Cultural Norms

Ask: Do I truly believe in this, or was I conditioned to accept it?

Study other cultures, philosophies, and unconventional lifestyles.

Avoid Decision-Making Based on Fear of Judgment

Understand that people's opinions are shaped by their own biases and insecurities.

Make decisions based on what aligns with your personal values, not what others expect.

Surround Yourself with Independent Thinkers

Spend time with people who encourage critical thinking, risk-taking, and personal growth.

Distance yourself from those who enforce conformity.

5.3 Overcoming Emotional Traps in Decision-Making

<u>How Emotions Hijack Rational Thinking</u>

Fear, anxiety, and excitement can cloud judgment.

Emotional decisions often lead to regret because they are reactive, not deliberate.

<u>Practical Ways to Reduce Emotional Bias</u>

Use the 10/10/10 Rule

Ask: How will I feel about this decision in 10 minutes, 10 months, and 10 years?

Helps separate short-term emotions from long-term consequences.

Delay Major Decisions

When emotional, wait 24 hours before acting.

This allows logical reasoning to take over impulsive thinking.

Journal Before Big Choices

Write down:

Why you want to make this decision

What fears are influencing you

What evidence supports your choice

Seeing thoughts on paper reduces emotional bias.

Identify Emotional Triggers

Recognize what environments, people, or situations make you react irrationally.

Example: If you overspend when stressed, develop alternative coping mechanisms.

5.4 Designing an Intentional Life of Freedom

Regaining control isn't just about making better decisions—it's about creating a life structure that supports long-term independence.

<u>How to Build a Life That Maximizes Freedom</u>

Control Your Time

Time is the ultimate form of freedom—without it, you are trapped.

Eliminate unnecessary obligations and prioritize tasks that bring fulfillment.

Achieve Financial Independence

Diversify income streams to avoid reliance on a single employer.

Live below your means so money doesn't dictate your choices.

Practice Essentialism

Avoid overcommitment—learn to say no to things that don't serve your long-term goals.

Keep life simple and focused on what truly matters.

Create Personal Freedom Rules

Define your own rules for success, decision-making, and lifestyle.

Example: Instead of following traditional career paths, create a rule like "I will only work on projects that excite me and align with my values."

Prioritize Health & Mental Clarity

Poor health limits freedom—your decisions become dictated by fatigue, illness, or stress.

Invest in exercise, meditation, and proper sleep to maintain physical and mental autonomy.

5.5 Daily Habits for Maintaining Control Over Your Decisions

True freedom is built on consistent habits that reinforce independence.

<u>Daily Practices to Stay in Control</u>

Morning Reflection (10 Minutes)

Ask: What choices do I want to make today that align with my goals?

Helps set clear daily intentions.

The 3-Decision Rule

Every day, focus on making three key decisions that align with your personal freedom.

Example: "I will say no to distractions, invest in learning, and choose progress over perfection."

Minimal Digital Consumption

Limit passive scrolling, news intake, and external influences.

Consume content with purpose rather than mindless engagement.

End-of-Day Self-Audit

Reflect on decisions:

Did I make choices that aligned with my values?

What influenced me today—my own goals or external forces?

Conclusion: The Path to Lasting Control

Regaining control isn't about eliminating all influences—that's impossible. Instead, it's about recognizing external pressures, overcoming emotional traps, and implementing structured habits that help you make deliberate, intentional choices.

Final Key Takeaways

? Use mental models to make clear, rational decisions.

? Reduce external influence from society, media, and toxic environments.

? Overcome emotional bias by delaying decisions and using logic-based frameworks.

? Design a life of autonomy by taking control of time, money, and habits.

? Implement daily practices to sustain freedom and independent thinking.

True freedom is not about rejecting all constraints—it's about mastering them and making choices with full awareness, clarity, and intention.

Spirituality & Purpose: Blind Faith vs. Enlightened Thinking

CHAPTER FORTY-ONE

The Foundations of Spirituality and Purpose

1.1 Understanding Spirituality & Purpose

<u>Defining Spirituality</u>

Spirituality is a deeply personal and complex aspect of human existence. It transcends religious beliefs and rituals, encompassing a sense of connection to something greater than oneself. While spirituality is often linked to faith and religion, it can also be an independent pursuit of meaning, peace, and enlightenment. It is an ongoing journey that allows individuals to seek purpose, fulfillment, and personal growth.

Historically, spirituality has been associated with organized religion, but in modern times, it has evolved into a broader concept that includes mindfulness, self-awareness, and a quest for inner peace. Some find spirituality through prayer and worship, while others explore it through meditation, philosophical inquiry, or nature. Regardless of the path, spirituality fosters a deeper understanding of life, existence, and one's place in the universe.

<u>The Role of Purpose in Spirituality</u>

Purpose is the driving force behind human actions and decisions. It provides direction, motivation, and fulfillment. A strong sense of purpose can lead to greater resilience, emotional well-being, and a sense of belonging. Spirituality often serves as a foundation for defining one's purpose, whether through religious doctrines, moral principles, or personal introspection.

A person's purpose can evolve over time, influenced by experiences, challenges, and personal growth. Some derive their sense of purpose from serving others, creating art, or pursuing knowledge, while others find it in devotion to a higher power. Understanding one's purpose requires self-reflection and an open mind to explore different philosophies and perspectives.

<u>The Connection Between Spirituality and Purpose</u>

The relationship between spirituality and purpose is symbiotic. Spirituality provides a lens through which individuals can interpret their experiences and struggles, while purpose gives direction to spiritual exploration. When both elements align, individuals often experience a profound sense of fulfillment and clarity.

For some, purpose emerges from religious teachings that provide a predefined path to follow. For others, it arises from personal experiences that lead to self-discovery. Regardless of the origin, purpose driven by spirituality encourages individuals to lead meaningful lives, cultivate positive relationships, and contribute to the well-being of society.

1.2 Faith: Blind or Enlightened?

<u>The Nature of Faith</u>

Faith is often described as a belief in something without tangible proof. It can be religious, philosophical, or even secular. Faith allows individuals to navigate uncertainty, providing comfort and stability in challenging times. However, faith can manifest in two distinct ways: blind faith and enlightened thinking.

<u>Blind Faith vs. Enlightened Thinking</u>

Blind faith refers to an unquestioning belief in doctrines, ideologies, or traditions without critical examination. It discourages doubt, curiosity, and rational analysis. While blind faith can offer immediate comfort and a sense of belonging, it can also lead to dogmatism, intolerance, and resistance to new ideas.

Enlightened thinking, on the other hand, encourages questioning, learning, and evolving perspectives. It allows individuals to embrace faith while remaining open to new insights. Enlightened thinkers analyze their beliefs, seek knowledge from multiple sources, and adapt their understanding as they grow.

For example, in history, many scientific discoveries were initially met with resistance due to blind faith in established doctrines. However, as enlightened thinking prevailed, societies evolved, leading to progress in medicine, technology, and human rights. Similarly, an enlightened approach to spirituality encourages individuals to explore their beliefs critically rather than accept them without question.

<u>Case Studies: Historical Examples</u>

Galileo Galilei and the Church: Galileo's advocacy for heliocentrism challenged the widely accepted geocentric view backed by religious authorities. Despite facing persecution, his work laid the foundation for modern astronomy.

The Reformation Movement: Martin Luther questioned the authority of the Catholic Church, leading to the Protestant Reformation, which emphasized personal interpretation of scripture rather than blind adherence to church doctrine.

Swami Vivekananda: He combined spirituality with rational thought, encouraging individuals to seek self-realization through knowledge, introspection, and experience rather than unquestioning faith.

These examples highlight the importance of questioning established beliefs to foster growth and enlightenment.

1.3 The Evolution of Spiritual Thought

<u>Ancient Spiritual Traditions</u>

Spirituality has been an integral part of human history, evolving from early animistic beliefs to organized religions and philosophical inquiries. In ancient times, spirituality was deeply intertwined with nature, mythology, and communal rituals. People sought to understand their existence through stories, symbols, and divine beings.

For instance:

Hinduism, one of the oldest spiritual traditions, emphasizes self-inquiry, karma, and dharma as paths to enlightenment.

Buddhism advocates mindfulness, compassion, and the pursuit of Nirvana through self-awareness rather than blind devotion.

Indigenous spiritual practices around the world celebrate the interconnectedness of all living beings and the sacredness of nature.

<u>The Impact of Philosophy and Reason</u>

As civilizations progressed, philosophy began to shape spiritual thought. Greek philosophers such as Socrates, Plato, and Aristotle introduced critical thinking and ethical inquiry, influencing religious and spiritual traditions worldwide.

Socrates encouraged questioning beliefs to arrive at deeper truths.

Plato explored the nature of the soul and the existence of a higher reality.

Aristotle emphasized logic and empirical evidence in understanding the world.

Similarly, in the East, Confucianism and Taoism emphasized harmony, ethics, and balance, influencing spiritual perspectives in China and beyond.

<u>The Modern Shift Toward Personal Spirituality</u>

In contemporary times, spirituality has become more individualized. Many people seek spiritual fulfillment outside traditional religious institutions. Practices such as meditation, mindfulness, and self-reflection have gained popularity, allowing individuals to craft their own spiritual journeys.

The modern era has also seen a rise in interfaith dialogue, where different religious and spiritual traditions learn from each other. This exchange of ideas fosters a more inclusive approach to spirituality, encouraging people to embrace wisdom from diverse sources rather than adhering strictly to a single doctrine.

Additionally, scientific advancements have influenced spiritual perspectives. The study of consciousness, quantum physics, and psychology has opened new discussions on the nature of existence, the mind-body connection, and the potential for spiritual experiences to be understood through empirical research.

Conclusion

The foundations of spirituality and purpose are built on a dynamic interplay between faith, reason, and personal growth. While blind faith can provide comfort, it may also hinder intellectual and spiritual development. Enlightened thinking, on the other hand, allows individuals to explore their beliefs with an open mind, fostering deeper understanding and personal transformation.

As spirituality evolves, individuals are increasingly embracing a more personalized approach, blending ancient wisdom with modern insights. This shift enables people to seek purpose not through rigid doctrines but through conscious exploration, self-awareness, and a genuine quest for truth.

Ultimately, spirituality and purpose are deeply intertwined, guiding individuals toward a fulfilling life marked by wisdom, compassion, and an ever-evolving understanding of existence.

CHAPTER FORTY-TWO

BLIND FAITH – COMFORT OR CONFINEMENT?

2.1 The Psychology Behind Blind Faith

<u>Understanding the Nature of Blind Faith</u>

Blind faith can be defined as unwavering belief in a doctrine, ideology, or authority without questioning its validity or seeking evidence. It often arises from deep-seated psychological and sociocultural conditioning. While faith can provide emotional comfort and stability, blind faith can limit critical thinking, personal growth, and freedom of choice.

<u>Why Do People Follow Beliefs Unquestioningly?</u>

Several psychological factors contribute to blind faith, including:

Fear of the Unknown: Uncertainty and existential questions drive people to seek absolute answers, even at the cost of logic.

Cognitive Dissonance: The discomfort of holding conflicting beliefs leads individuals to accept doctrines without question to maintain mental consistency.

Group Conformity: Social and familial influence conditions individuals to accept beliefs without skepticism.

Emotional Security: Faith provides a sense of belonging, identity, and purpose, making it difficult to challenge established beliefs.

Authoritarian Influence: Charismatic leaders, religious institutions, or political ideologies reinforce adherence through persuasion and control.

<u>The Role of Fear and Control</u>

Blind faith is often rooted in fear—fear of divine punishment, societal rejection, or existential uncertainty. Throughout history, authoritative institutions have used this fear to exert control, discouraging dissent and critical inquiry. When individuals surrender personal agency in the name of faith, they may unknowingly confine themselves to rigid worldviews that limit their intellectual and spiritual growth.

2.2 The Pitfalls of Blind Faith

<u>Suppression of Critical Thinking</u>

Blind faith discourages questioning, exploration, and curiosity. When individuals accept doctrines without scrutiny, they miss opportunities for growth and broader understanding. This suppression of critical thinking can have serious consequences, such as:

Acceptance of misleading information without verification.

Resistance to scientific discoveries and rational explanations.

Perpetuation of outdated beliefs that hinder progress.

<u>Manipulation and Control</u>

Blind faith can be exploited by those in power to manipulate followers. Examples include:

Cults and Extremist Groups: Leaders instill unquestioning obedience, often leading followers toward destructive actions.

Fraudulent Gurus and Religious Leaders: Some exploit blind faith for financial gain, abuse, or personal influence.

Political and Social Manipulation: Ideological doctrines can be used to justify discrimination, oppression, or violence.

<u>When Faith Becomes a Barrier to Personal Growth</u>

While faith can offer comfort, blind faith may prevent individuals from exploring diverse perspectives and evolving their beliefs. Examples of this include:

Sticking to outdated traditions without questioning their relevance.

Rejecting new scientific or philosophical ideas out of fear.

Avoiding personal introspection and critical evaluation of beliefs.

By blindly adhering to doctrines, individuals may inadvertently confine themselves to rigid ideologies, reducing their capacity for self-improvement and a deeper understanding of life.

2.3 When Blind Faith Becomes Toxic

<u>Dogma vs. Open Spirituality</u>

Blind faith turns toxic when it fosters dogmatism—an uncompromising adherence to doctrine. Dogma can create division, intolerance, and even violence. Open spirituality, in contrast, encourages exploration, dialogue, and personal interpretation of faith.

<u>Faith-Based Conflicts and Extremism</u>

Throughout history, blind faith has fueled conflicts, including:

Religious wars, such as the Crusades and sectarian violence.

Persecution of dissenters, including scientific thinkers and reformers.

Acts of terrorism driven by ideological fanaticism.

<u>The Role of Blind Faith in Mass Hysteria</u>

Examples of blind faith-driven hysteria include:

Witch hunts and superstitious fear-based persecutions.

Unfounded conspiracy theories leading to societal paranoia.

The spread of misinformation due to uncritical acceptance of doctrine.

Blind faith, when unchecked, can become a powerful tool for mass manipulation, leading to destructive societal consequences.

2.4 The Dangers of Blind Faith in Modern Society

<u>Science and Rationality vs. Unquestioning Belief</u>

Blind faith often conflicts with scientific advancements and rational thought. Examples include:

Medical Science vs. Superstition: Faith healers or miracle cures that discourage seeking professional medical help.

Technology and Progress: Resistance to innovations due to traditional beliefs.

Misinformation in the Digital Age: The internet allows rapid spread of unverified claims, reinforced by blind faith in uncredible sources.

<u>The Challenge of Breaking Free from Blind Faith</u>

Breaking free from blind faith requires:

Encouraging critical thinking from an early age.

Promoting open discussions about faith and beliefs.

Allowing space for doubt and questioning without fear of ostracization.

Fostering an educational environment where individuals explore multiple perspectives.

2.5 The Balance Between Faith and Reason

<u>Can Faith Exist Without Being Blind?</u>

Faith and reason do not have to be mutually exclusive. A balanced approach allows for faith to be a source of strength while maintaining an open mind. This balance involves:

Acknowledging the limitations of human understanding while being open to new information.

Differentiating between faith based on experience and faith based on fear.

Using faith as a tool for self-discovery rather than an excuse to avoid critical thinking.

<u>Steps Toward Enlightened Thinking</u>

To transition from blind faith to enlightened thinking:

Cultivate Curiosity: Question beliefs, explore different perspectives, and seek knowledge.

Engage in Self-Reflection: Assess personal values and beliefs regularly.

Encourage Rational Discourse: Discuss faith with people of different viewpoints to challenge and refine understanding.

Educate Yourself Continuously: Stay informed about historical, scientific, and philosophical insights.

<u>Faith as a Source of Empowerment</u>

Faith can be a powerful source of hope and purpose when approached with awareness and flexibility. When individuals move beyond blind adherence and embrace faith as a means of growth, they cultivate a richer, more meaningful spiritual journey.

Conclusion

Blind faith offers comfort but can also act as a form of confinement, restricting growth, rational inquiry, and personal freedom. While faith can provide stability, it should not come at the cost of intellectual curiosity or individual autonomy. By embracing a balance between faith and reason, individuals can cultivate a more enlightened, fulfilling spiritual path.

Ultimately, spirituality should not be about unquestioning submission but about personal discovery, ethical exploration, and continuous growth. Faith, when combined with reason, leads to wisdom rather than confinement, allowing individuals to navigate life with both conviction and openness.

CHAPTER FORTY-THREE

ENLIGHTENED THINKING – THE POWER OF CONSCIOUS FAITH

3.1 What is Enlightened Thinking?

<u>Defining Enlightened Thinking</u>

Enlightened thinking is a conscious, reflective approach to faith and belief systems. It is the balance between faith and reason, where individuals actively engage with their spiritual beliefs rather than accepting them without question. Unlike blind faith, which relies on unquestioning obedience, enlightened thinking encourages exploration, self-awareness, and rational evaluation.

<u>The Interplay Between Faith, Logic, and Wisdom</u>

Faith and reason have often been portrayed as opposing forces, but enlightened thinking integrates the two. It acknowledges that faith provides meaning and purpose, while reason ensures clarity and intellectual honesty. Wisdom emerges when both are harmonized, enabling individuals to live with conviction while remaining open to growth and new perspectives.

<u>Characteristics of an Enlightened Thinker</u>

Curiosity: Always seeking to learn and expand knowledge.

Critical Thinking: Questioning beliefs rather than blindly accepting them.

Openness to Change: Willingness to adapt beliefs based on new evidence.

Empathy and Tolerance: Respecting different viewpoints while holding personal convictions.

Self-Reflection: Regularly evaluating personal beliefs and spiritual journey.

3.2 Spirituality as a Tool for Growth

<u>Seeking Meaning with Awareness</u>

Spirituality, when approached with awareness, becomes a tool for personal transformation. It helps individuals navigate life's challenges, find peace amid uncertainty, and develop resilience. Enlightened spirituality does not demand conformity but encourages each person to forge their own path.

<u>Embracing Uncertainty While Maintaining Purpose</u>

Unlike blind faith, which seeks absolute certainty, enlightened thinking accepts that some questions may not have definitive answers. This approach allows individuals to live purposefully without feeling threatened by doubt or ambiguity.

<u>Examples of Enlightened Spiritual Figures</u>

Buddha: Advocated for self-inquiry and mindfulness rather than rigid dogma.

Rumi: Encouraged spiritual exploration through poetry and personal experience.

Swami Vivekananda: Promoted rational faith and self-discovery within spirituality.

Albert Einstein: Valued the mystical experience of the universe while upholding scientific rigor.

Each of these figures demonstrated that faith and reason can coexist, shaping a deeper and more fulfilling understanding of life.

3.3 Science and Spirituality: Friends or Foes?

<u>The Intersection of Scientific Inquiry and Spiritual Experience</u>

Traditionally, science and spirituality have been seen as conflicting domains. However, modern advancements reveal an overlap between the two. Neuroscience, psychology, and physics increasingly explore spiritual experiences, consciousness, and interconnectedness.

<u>Scientific Studies on Meditation and Mindfulness</u>

Scientific research supports the benefits of spiritual practices such as meditation and mindfulness. Studies indicate that regular meditation can:

Reduce stress and anxiety.

Enhance cognitive function and emotional regulation.

Improve overall well-being and mental clarity.

<u>Quantum Physics and the Nature of Consciousness</u>

Quantum physics has introduced concepts that parallel spiritual insights:

Interconnectedness: Everything in the universe is fundamentally connected.

Observer Effect: Consciousness influences reality at the quantum level.

Multiple Realities: The idea that perception shapes experience aligns with certain spiritual traditions.

While science does not confirm religious doctrines, it offers insights that validate spiritual experiences and personal transformation.

3.4 Finding Purpose – A Conscious Journey

<u>Defining Your Own Purpose</u>

Purpose is not something imposed by external authorities but discovered through self-reflection and conscious living. Enlightened thinkers recognize that purpose evolves and is shaped by personal experiences, relationships, and aspirations.

<u>Differentiating Societal Expectations from True Calling</u>

Many people inherit beliefs about purpose from culture, religion, and society. However, enlightened thinking challenges individuals to distinguish between external pressures and their authentic inner calling. This involves:

Identifying personal values.

Understanding strengths and passions.

Aligning daily actions with long-term fulfillment.

Aligning Purpose with Personal Values and Spirituality

Purpose should be rooted in authenticity and integrity. It is not about seeking validation but living in accordance with one's highest principles. Enlightened spirituality provides a framework for individuals to pursue purpose in a way that contributes to both personal growth and collective well-being.

3.5 Overcoming Internal and External Challenges

<u>Handling Doubt and Uncertainty in Faith</u>

Doubt is a natural part of an enlightened spiritual journey. Rather than seeing doubt as a weakness, enlightened thinkers use it as an opportunity for deeper understanding. Strategies to embrace doubt include:

Engaging in philosophical and theological discussions.

Exploring multiple perspectives through literature and debate.

Practicing mindfulness to stay grounded amid uncertainty.

<u>Dealing with Societal Pressure Regarding Spiritual Beliefs</u>

Many individuals face external pressure to conform to traditional beliefs. Overcoming this challenge involves:

Developing confidence in personal convictions.

Building a supportive community of like-minded thinkers.

Respecting others' beliefs while asserting one's autonomy.

<u>Creating a Flexible Yet Meaningful Belief System</u>

A rigid belief system can be limiting, whereas a flexible approach allows for growth and adaptation. Enlightened thinking encourages:

Integrating wisdom from various traditions and disciplines.

Adjusting beliefs in light of new experiences and insights.

Allowing room for continuous learning and transformation.

Conclusion: The Power of Conscious Faith

Enlightened thinking is about embracing faith with awareness, reason, and self-reflection. It moves beyond blind adherence to doctrine and fosters a deeper, more meaningful connection with spirituality. By combining faith and reason, individuals cultivate a balanced perspective that leads to wisdom, purpose, and inner peace.

Ultimately, enlightened spirituality is not about possessing all the answers but about living with an open heart and mind, continuously seeking truth, growth, and harmony in the journey of life.

CHAPTER FORTY-FOUR

FINDING PURPOSE – A CONSCIOUS JOURNEY

4.1 Defining Your Own Purpose

<u>Understanding Purpose in Life</u>

Purpose is often considered the guiding force behind human actions, emotions, and aspirations. It is what gives life meaning and motivates individuals to strive for fulfillment. While some find purpose in relationships, careers, or spirituality, others seek it in personal growth, creativity, or service to humanity.

Purpose is not a fixed concept; it evolves as individuals gain experience, encounter challenges, and develop a deeper understanding of themselves and the world around them.

<u>Why Is Purpose Important?</u>

A strong sense of purpose leads to:

Greater resilience in the face of adversity.

Higher levels of motivation and productivity.

Improved mental and emotional well-being.

Stronger social connections and relationships.

A sense of fulfillment and satisfaction in life.

Finding purpose is not about achieving a singular goal; rather, it is about aligning daily actions with deeper values and intentions.

4.2 Methods to Cultivate Enlightened Spirituality

1. Self-Reflection and Introspection

Self-reflection is a crucial step in identifying one's purpose. It involves asking deep questions about personal values, motivations, and aspirations. Journaling, meditation, and quiet contemplation can help uncover insights about one's purpose.

Questions for self-reflection:

What activities make me feel most fulfilled?

What values are most important to me?

How do I want to contribute to the world?

What challenges have shaped my beliefs and goals?

2. Engaging in Meaningful Experiences

Experiencing life beyond routine obligations allows individuals to explore new passions and perspectives. Traveling, volunteering, and learning new skills can broaden one's understanding of what brings joy and fulfillment.

3. The Role of Mindfulness and Presence

Practicing mindfulness enables individuals to focus on the present moment rather than being consumed by past regrets or future anxieties. A mindful approach to life enhances clarity and awareness, making it easier to recognize what aligns with one's true purpose.

4.3 Overcoming Internal and External Challenges

<u>Handling Self-Doubt and Fear</u>

Many people struggle with self-doubt when seeking purpose. Fear of failure, judgment, or uncertainty can hinder progress. Overcoming these fears involves:

Accepting that uncertainty is a natural part of life.

Reframing failure as a learning experience.

Trusting the process of self-discovery.

<u>Dealing with Societal Expectations</u>

Societal norms and cultural expectations can often dictate what a 'meaningful' life should look like. However, an individual's true purpose may not align with conventional paths. Strategies to navigate this include:

Defining success based on personal values rather than societal standards.

Seeking support from like-minded individuals.

Setting boundaries against external pressures.

Managing Transitions and Shifts in Purpose

As people grow, their purpose may shift. Career changes, life events, or evolving beliefs may lead to new directions. Embracing change with openness and curiosity is key to maintaining a fulfilling journey.

4.4 Aligning Purpose with Personal Values and Spirituality

<u>The Connection Between Purpose and Spirituality</u>

Spirituality often plays a role in shaping one's purpose by providing a sense of interconnectedness and moral guidance. Whether through religious faith, philosophical inquiry, or mindfulness practices, spirituality helps individuals understand their role in the broader scheme of life.

<u>Identifying Core Values</u>

Aligning purpose with values ensures authenticity and consistency. Common core values include:

Compassion and service to others.

Creativity and self-expression.

Knowledge and continuous learning.

Adventure and exploration.

Family and relationships.

<u>Integrating Purpose into Daily Life</u>

Living with purpose does not always require grand achievements. Small, intentional actions that align with one's values can be equally meaningful. Ways to integrate purpose into daily life include:

Practicing gratitude and appreciation.

Engaging in acts of kindness.

Pursuing work that aligns with one's passions.

Maintaining a balanced and intentional lifestyle.

4.5 The Lifelong Journey of Purpose Discovery

<u>Embracing Change and Growth</u>

Understanding that purpose is not static but dynamic allows individuals to remain adaptable and open to new opportunities. Life's experiences continuously shape and refine one's purpose.

<u>Learning from Role Models and Mentors</u>

Observing and learning from others who have found meaningful purpose can provide inspiration and guidance. Role models can be historical figures, spiritual leaders, or everyday individuals who embody wisdom and fulfillment.

<u>Creating a Personal Purpose Statement</u>

A purpose statement is a concise declaration of one's intentions and guiding principles. Crafting a personal purpose statement involves:

<u>Summarizing key values and passions.</u>

Defining how one wishes to contribute to the world.

Revisiting and refining the statement as life evolves.

Example: "I strive to inspire and uplift others through creativity and education, fostering a community of learning and personal growth."

Conclusion

Finding purpose is a conscious and evolving journey. It requires self-reflection, openness to change, and the courage to align actions with personal values. By embracing both spiritual wisdom and rational inquiry, individuals can cultivate a life rich in meaning and fulfillment. Purpose is not a destination but a way of being—one that continues to evolve with each experience and insight gained along the way.

CHAPTER FORTY-FIVE

THE FUTURE OF SPIRITUALITY AND PURPOSE

5.1 The Rise of Individualized Spirituality

<u>Moving Away from Organized Religion</u>

In the past, spirituality was largely defined by organized religions, with established doctrines and communal practices. However, in the modern era, more individuals are shifting toward personalized spirituality. This shift is characterized by:

A decline in traditional religious affiliation.

Increased interest in personal spiritual experiences.

A focus on inner growth rather than external rituals.

<u>The Role of Technology in Spiritual Exploration</u>

Technology has provided unprecedented access to spiritual knowledge, connecting individuals across the globe. Key influences include:

Online courses, guided meditations, and virtual communities.

AI-driven spiritual coaching and personalized self-help tools.

Digital libraries of ancient and modern spiritual texts.

As technology continues to evolve, it will likely play a greater role in shaping personal spirituality, making it more accessible and customizable.

5.2 How Society Shapes Faith and Purpose

<u>The Influence of Culture and Education</u>

As societies become more globalized, exposure to diverse spiritual traditions has increased. This has led to:

The blending of various spiritual philosophies.

Greater acceptance of interfaith dialogue.

The rise of secular spirituality, where purpose is sought outside of religious contexts.

Education also plays a significant role in shaping faith. Schools and universities now incorporate mindfulness, ethics, and philosophy into curricula, encouraging critical thinking about spirituality and purpose.

<u>Spirituality and Mental Health</u>

The recognition of spirituality's role in mental health has grown in recent years. Practices such as meditation, gratitude journaling, and mindful breathing are now recommended alongside conventional psychological treatments.

Spiritual well-being has been linked to:

Reduced stress and anxiety.

Increased emotional resilience.

Greater overall life satisfaction.

5.3 The Impact of Scientific Discoveries on Spiritual Thought

<u>Neuroscience and Consciousness</u>

Advances in neuroscience have provided insights into spiritual experiences. Brain imaging studies reveal that meditation, prayer, and deep contemplation activate specific neural networks associated with:

Emotional regulation.

A sense of interconnectedness.

Heightened states of awareness.

This scientific approach to spirituality validates ancient wisdom while encouraging new ways to explore consciousness.

<u>The Exploration of the Universe and Existence</u>

Astrophysics and quantum mechanics continue to challenge traditional views on existence. Concepts such as:

The multiverse theory.

The observer effect in quantum physics.

The nature of dark matter and dark energy.

These discoveries provoke deep philosophical and spiritual questions, leading to renewed discussions about the nature of reality, divinity, and human purpose.

5.4 The Evolution of Purpose in a Changing World

<u>The Intersection of Spirituality and Artificial Intelligence</u>

With artificial intelligence increasingly influencing daily life, new ethical and existential questions arise:

Can AI possess consciousness or spirituality?

How does AI influence human purpose?

Will spirituality evolve as technology advances?

The answers to these questions will likely shape the future of spirituality, leading to new philosophical frameworks and interpretations of consciousness.

<u>Purpose in a Postmodern World</u>

Modern society is characterized by rapid change, uncertainty, and increasing complexity. As traditional paths to purpose (such as religion and lifelong careers) become less dominant, individuals are seeking:

Meaning through personal passions and creativity.

Community-driven spiritual experiences.

Ecological and humanitarian activism as spiritual expressions.

This shift suggests that purpose will continue to diversify, with each individual crafting their unique meaning in life.

5.5 Creating a Future-Ready Spiritual Framework

<u>The Need for Flexible Spirituality</u>

In the future, spirituality will likely emphasize adaptability and openness. Characteristics of a future-ready spiritual framework include:

The ability to integrate new knowledge and insights.

A focus on experiential spirituality rather than rigid dogma.

Inclusivity and acceptance of diverse spiritual paths.

<u>Practices for Lifelong Spiritual Enlightenment</u>

To remain spiritually engaged in an evolving world, individuals can cultivate:

Continuous Learning: Exploring spiritual traditions, philosophy, and science.

Meditation and Mindfulness: Strengthening self-awareness and inner peace.

Community Involvement: Engaging in discussions and practices that promote collective growth.

<u>Encouraging Critical Thinking While Maintaining Purpose</u>

A future-oriented approach to spirituality encourages:

Questioning and analyzing spiritual beliefs.

Balancing faith with reason and scientific understanding.

Allowing for both doubt and conviction in one's journey.

Conclusion: The Ongoing Journey of Spirituality and Purpose

The future of spirituality and purpose is dynamic and ever-evolving. As human understanding deepens through science, technology, and personal introspection, spirituality will continue to adapt. The challenge ahead is to embrace this evolution with openness, ensuring that faith and purpose remain meaningful, relevant, and enriching in the changing landscape of human existence.

By integrating wisdom from both ancient traditions and modern advancements, individuals can navigate their spiritual journeys with a balanced approach—one that fosters both personal fulfillment and a broader sense of interconnectedness with the world.

The Life Audit Framework: A Fraud Examiner's Approach To Personal Growth

<u>Summary of Lessons & Key Takeaways</u>

Throughout this book, we've explored the red flags that appear in different areas of life—health, relationships, career, finances, decision-making, and personal growth—and how they mirror the warning signs of fraud. We've also learned how self-deception can lead us down dangerous paths and how recognizing patterns early can prevent long-term damage.

In this final chapter, we'll consolidate everything into a practical toolkit—one that you can use to audit your life, make better decisions, and avoid self-sabotage.

Step 1: Identifying the Red Flags in Your Life

? Physical Health – Am I ignoring symptoms, making excuses, or relying on quick fixes?

? Mental & Emotional Well-being – Do I engage in negative self-talk, suppress emotions, or avoid difficult truths?

? Love & Relationships – Are my relationships nurturing or draining? Do I overlook red flags in romantic or familial ties?

? Friendships & Social Circles – Are the people around me adding value or causing harm?

? Career & Professional Growth – Am I in a fulfilling career, or am I tolerating a toxic work environment?

? Financial Stability – Am I making sound financial decisions, or am I indulging in risky behavior?

? Decision-Making & Personal Freedom – Am I truly in control of my choices, or am I being influenced/manipulated?

? Spirituality & Purpose – Am I being guided by genuine beliefs, or am I falling for misleading ideologies?

? ACTION: Write down the red flags you recognize in these areas. Awareness is the first step to change.

Step 2: Conducting a Personal Audit

A fraud examiner investigates financial reports for inconsistencies. You can do the same for your life.

? Ask Yourself These Questions:

✓ What patterns keep repeating in my life? (Bad financial decisions, toxic relationships, unhealthy habits?)

✔ Where am I self-sabotaging? (Ignoring advice, delaying action, avoiding discomfort?)

✔ Who influences my decisions? (Am I easily swayed by others?)

✔ Where do I lack discipline? (Is it my health, career, or finances?)

? ACTION: Pick one area of your life and perform a detailed audit using these questions.

Step 3: Building Internal Controls for Life

Fraud prevention isn't about fixing problems after they happen—it's about putting safeguards in place to stop them before they spiral out of control.

? For Physical Health – Implement daily tracking (food, workouts, sleep) to catch unhealthy patterns early.

? For Mental Health – Practice mindfulness, journaling, and therapy to challenge negative thoughts.

? For Relationships – Set boundaries to avoid being emotionally manipulated.

? For Career – Regularly assess job satisfaction and professional growth.

? For Finances – Stick to budgeting, financial audits, and investment due diligence.

? For Decision-Making – Pause before making impulsive choices; seek second opinions when necessary.

? ACTION: Set up 3 personal controls that will help you prevent self-sabotage in different areas.

Step 4: Learning to Trust but Verify

In fraud detection, "Trust but Verify" is a golden rule. In life, balance trust with critical thinking to avoid being deceived—whether by people, circumstances, or your own mind.

✔ Trust your instincts, but don't ignore logic.

✔ Verify facts before making big decisions.

✔ Evaluate relationships over time, not just based on words.

✔ Double-check your financial choices before committing.

? ACTION: The next time you make a big decision, ask yourself: "Am I acting on emotion or logic?"

Step 5: Continuous Growth – The Ongoing Audit of Life

? Fraud happens when oversight stops. The same goes for personal growth—if you stop checking in with yourself, old patterns will creep back in.

? How to keep yourself accountable:

? Perform quarterly life audits – Just like companies do financial audits, take time every few months to reflect, reset, and reassess.

? Have an accountability system – Share your goals with a mentor, friend, or coach.

? Keep learning – Stay open to self-improvement, therapy, and personal development.

? ACTION: Set a date in your calendar for your next personal audit.

Final Thoughts: You Are Your Own Fraud Examiner

This book was never about preventing fraud in business—it was about preventing self-sabotage in life.

The biggest scams aren't just financial—they happen when we:

? Ignore red flags in our health, relationships, or careers.

? Lie to ourselves about our habits and decisions.

? Assume we'll "fix things later" instead of taking action now.

But the good news? Once you start recognizing patterns, you can change them.

✓ Awareness is your best defense.

✓ Self-auditing keeps you honest.

✓ Internal controls keep you from repeating mistakes.

Fraud detection saves companies from financial collapse. Applying the same principles to life can save you from unnecessary setbacks, regret, and wasted time.

So from now on, treat your life like an ongoing audit. Pay attention to the signs. Act before the damage is done. And above all, trust yourself—but always verify.

Because the best way to navigate the lows in life?

Never let the red flags go unnoticed again.